T0095101

The Silver Secret of Caballo Bay

By
EAC Troy R. Cole Sr. USN Ret.

Corregidor and Caballo Islands at the entrance
to Manila Bay, Luzon, Philippine Islands

Order this book online at www.trafford.com
or email orders@trafford.com

Most Trafford titles are also available at major online book retailers.

© Copyright 2011 EAC Troy R. Cole Sr. USN Ret..
All rights reserved. No part of this publication may be reproduced, stored in a retrieval
system, or transmitted, in any form or by any means, electronic, mechanical, photocopying,
recording, or otherwise, without the written prior permission of the author.

Printed in the United States of America.

ISBN: 978-1-4269-5534-1 (sc)
ISBN: 978-1-4269-6222-6 (hc)
ISBN: 978-1-4269-6223-3 (e)

Library of Congress Control Number: 2011900792

Trafford rev. 03/16/2011

 www.trafford.com

North America & International
toll-free: 1 888 232 4444 (USA & Canada)
phone: 250 383 6864 ♦ fax: 812 355 4082

This story is respectfully dedicated to all Officers and Enlisted men of the United States Navy who served on Net Tenders during World War 11 and after. Also to all Navy and Army divers that made this story possible.

By

EAC Troy R. Cole Sr. USN Ret.

Acknowledgments

Few books or stories are ever the work of a single author. This one is certainly no exception. That line is from the Navy's Bluejacket's Manual. My thanks to all the web sites I used and to all the logs from all the ships in this story. My special thanks goes to the great books and articles I have used for references.

My thanks to my shipmates on the U.S.S. Silverbell AN-51

Mrs. Deb Kadair a fifth grade teacher and author at the Parkside Elementary School, Georgetown, Texas.

Mr. Garry Lee Byerly of Liberty Hill, Texas, who help me with all the pictures for the story.

Article by Milton J. Meehan (Moose) RDM 2/c, of Newport Beach, California.

Doctor Lawrence W. Kerkow of Universal City, Texas, for taking the time to review my story.

Amanda M. McCoy Impress Supervisor, of Production at Store #1416 Office Max Inc, Cedar Park, Texas.

The Silver Secret of Caballo Bay

By
EAC Troy R. Cole Sr. USN Ret.

Corregidor and Caballo Island, Caballo Inland is the smaller of the two Islands;
Caballo Bay is on the North side of the Island.

Our story starts and ends
in the area between the two Islands.

The events of this story begin on December 8th, 1941 a few hours after the Japanese attack on Pearl Harbor, Territory of Hawaii, on December 7th, 1941. It is the 8th of December in the Philippines due to the International Date Line or the 180th Standard Parallel.

At this time the military in the Philippines was about (170,000) combined American and Philippine troops and they were scattered in various locations throughout the Philippine Islands. The entire Philippines Islands consisted of around (7,107) islands with around

(4,000) islands inhabited. Over the next three weeks these forces were to lose ground to overwhelming Japanese forces on a daily basis. By December 23rd, 1941 Manila, the Philippine Capitol, was declared an open city. This was done to help keep the building destruction and death of civilians down.

The US Army Intelligence Bureau (G-2) was to arrange for the transportation of the Philippine National Treasury and contents of the Philippine Central Bank to the relative safety of Corregidor Island.

Note:

One man in December of 1941 from the Treasury Department a Reynolds North, banker by trade was assigned to go to Manila. His job was to remove the vast horde of securities, consisting of gold and silver coined money and bullion, along with bearer bonds, treasury certificates, precious stones, as well as privately held gold items and mementos, made it to the island, but with great many exertions and hardships on the part of many individuals.

The Government securities alone consisted of over (51) tons of gold bullion, (32) tons of silver bullion, (140) tons of silver pesos and centavos, and millions of paper treasury notes, bonds and corporations stocks. Why was the Treasury Department was involved? The bank of Manila was still control by the United States. The civilian property, otherwise known as "private holdings", consisted of approximately two tons of gold bullion in various size ingots, along with an unknown amount of priceless stones and foreign currency. When orders were received to evacuate the city, many of the paper inventories records were still incomplete, with many private citizens not even being given receipts for their valuables.

2nd January 1942, Manila was declared an open city to save the building and the people.

At one point just prior to the city's evacuation, the old part of Manila within the old Fort Santiago area had been severely bombed during a Japanese air raid. The storage rooms of the rather large holdings of silver pesos was hit, scattering the crated and bagged coins through the room, clerks were inundated and actually buried with silver coins for a short time. However, it didn't take long for the Treasury workers to re-pack the coins for shipment.

The treasury staff appropriated what vessels they could lay their hands on for transportation of securities to Corregidor, which consisted mostly of outdated US Navy harbor tugs and barges, plus small civilian boats and larger Navy vessels including a US Army vessel. Some of the vessels used in this operation were the USS Canopus (AS-9) a submarine tender, the USS Pigeon (ASR-6) a minesweeper and the US Army Mineplanter the USAMP Harrison.

U.S.S. Pigeon (ASR-6) a (Minesweeper) Sank on the 4th May 1942, by Japanese Dive Bombers.

The U.S. Army Mineplanter (USAMP) Harrison was named after General George Harrison the first American governor of the Philippines.

The USS Canopus (AS-9), (a submarine tender) (On April 9th 1942) was scuttled in deep water off Bataan.
Named after the brightest star in the southern hemisphere.

Note:

At the entrance to Manila bay a fort made of concrete that looked like a ship stood guard at the entrance for years. This ship is called Fort Drum and it rests on El Fraile Island. This note had to be put in the story as anyone entering Manila Bay has to pass by Fort Drum. The picture below is Fort Drum in 1940. Left side of the picture is the bow, looking at the South China Sea.

Fort Drum before World War 11.

Fort Drum after World War 11. Destroyed by Japanese aircraft. Bow is pointed at the South China Sea.

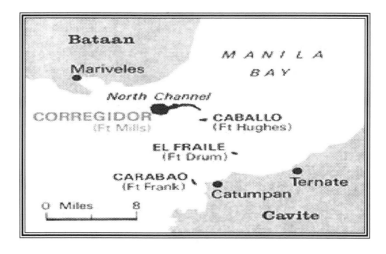

Map showing entrance to, Manila Bay, and the famous Islands at the entrance.

Some of the smaller civilian craft were the "Don Esteban" and the presidential yacht "Casiano" which received a rather substantial shipment of silver ingots and pesos. The Government gold bars loaded onto these vessels and the cargo alone was worth 41 million dollars US, (at $32.00 US per. oz.).

Note: The presidential yacht the "Casiano" was sunk by Japanese aircraft on January 26th, 1942.

In general, ingots, coins, and other precious metals were stuffed into footlockers, metal cabinets, and any other container that could take the weight. The containers were then thrown down abruptly onto the decks of the small fleet. The loading process took four days to complete and <u>was done only at night due to the constant, bombing raids.</u> They bombed the area around the city only during the daylight hours. With the loading completed, the small fleet sailed down the Manila Bay headed for Corregidor Island at night on December 27th, 1941.

The North Dock same as it was in 1941, except for the small craft alongside the dock.
Bataan is in the background

Upon arrival at the island's North Dock the small vessels had a difficult time maneuvering for pier space among the larger supply ships. As a result, each boat would pull up, place its cargo containers onto the dock, and then vacate the space for the next boat in line to repeat the procedure. In this manner it took two nights and one day to deliver the valuables from the North Dock to the two designated "vault" areas on Corregidor Island.

North Dock was piled high with Ammunition boxes, gas cans, food and medical supplies and the Philippine National Treasury securities. The US Army personnel were cooperative in assisting to move the many containers of wealth but they naturally considered gold and silver less important than weapons and ammunition. At that time Corregidor was not under direct assault, but the defenders knew that it was only a matter of time and getting caught with a pier full of open containers of fuel, food and the treasure would not have been a welcome situation.

In a relatively short time, however, the (140) tons of silver pesos were packed in canvas bags, put in wooden crates and transported safely from the dock to the US Navy section of the large underground complex known as the Malinta Tunnels. Well over (15) million silver pesos and centavo coins were catalogued in the Navy tunnels. The treasure stowed in the canvas bags, each bag containing (2,000) pesos ($1,000 US). The rest were then placed in wooden boxes, which measured (14 inches by 14 inches by 24 inches), each holding three bags or (6,000) pesos ($3,000 US) per box. The boxes weighed about (300) pounds each.

Looking at entrance to Malinta tunnel.

Inside Malinta tunnel.

On February 3rd, 1942 the United States sub a "Tambor" class submarine.

The "USS Trout (SS 202) arrived just outside San Jose Bay, and was met by a United States Navy ship the USS Pigeon (ASR-6) and was then escorted through the mine field to Corregidor,s South Dock. Here she offloaded her much needed cargo and medical supplies.

After the unloading was completed the Commanding Officer of the Trout requested some type of ballast from Corregidor dock party so his sub would be able to dive quickly upon leaving the area. During a brief conference with the officer in charge at the dock it was decided that the Captain of the Trout and one Officer, would hold a quick meeting with the Command Staff. It was mutually agreed that this would be the perfect opportunity to ship out at least part of the Philippine National Securities from the Island. The Treasury staff were awakened and brought to the South Dock.

South dock as it was in 1941.

The U.S.S. Trout (SS 202) coming alongside the U.S.S. Detroit (CL-8). The U.S.S. Trout (SS 202)
sank by Japanese Destroyer in 1944, with all 81 hands.

Two trucks were quickly sent up to the vault at the stockade on Middleside (*named after the middle area of the Island*) to bring a shipment down to the South Dock. The two tons worth of "Private Gold" ingots, worth over two million dollars and eighteen tons of silver pesos valued at ($360,000) dollars were placed in the bilges of the Trout. This was part of the treasure hidden by the authorities prior to the Japanese occupation of Manila. All available gold bullion, silver pesos, Philippine Securities, and all official US documents had been transported to the caves of Corregidor for safekeeping. The only portion of the treasure evacuated from Corregidor was this unplanned cargo carried by the Trout.

The U.S.S. Trout (SS202), now a submersible "National bank", proceeded on her regular war time patrol around the outer Philippine Islands. Since the Commanding Officer of the Trout had no orders other than to proceed on a regular patrol, he did not head directly back to Pearl Harbor, Oahu, Territory of Hawaii. He maneuvered his sub towards Mindanao and eventually sank two Japanese vessels before heading home. After the arrival of the sub at Pearl Harbor, the U.S.S. Trout (SS202) pulled alongside the light cruiser the U.S.S. Detroit (CL-8) and off loaded her precious cargo, which was eventually transported safely to the United States mint storage facilities in San Francisco, California.

U. S.S. Detroit (CL-8)

The U.S.S. Trout (SS 202) tied alongside the U.S.S. Detroit (CL-8) off loading gold bars
onto
her decks at Pearl Harbor, Territory of Hawaii.

Gold bars on deck of the U.S.S. Trout (SS 202) March 1942.

The U.S.S. Detroit (CL-8) finished her outstanding service in the in the U.S. Navy at the Philadelphia Navy Yard, were she was decommissioned on the 11th January 1946. The fate of the U.S.S. Trout (SS202), while on patrol in 1944 she was sunk with (81) hands. Her death was the result of 19 to 20 depth charges from a Japanese destroyer screening a convoy. Info on the demise of the Trout comes from Japanese Navy records.

After the surrender of Bataan on 9th April, it was obvious that Corregidor's days were numbered. Excess material such as submarine spare parts, torpedoes, rifles, ammunition, pistols, etc. were destroyed or dumped into the sea to prevent them from falling into enemy hands. The treasure that had by far the greatest value was the (350) tons of silver pesos. The idea of blowing up the caves was quickly abandoned in favor of a proposal to make recovery of the silver considerably more difficult for the Japanese. This was done by dumping the silver in deep water off Caballo Bay, which lies South of the of Corregidor and is formed by the crescent shaped tail of this Island and nearby Caballo Island. It was ideally suited for this purpose. The water in the central part of the bay is around (20) fathoms, and the main mountainous bulk of Corregidor to the North provided some protection against observation by the Japanese on Bataan.

6th May 1942 The USS Pigeon (ASR-6), and barge and Army Mineplanter the (USAMP) Harrison, with barge in tow, were loaded with wooden boxes that were full of the silver pesos in canvas bags and then taken out to Caballo Bay and jettisoned into the bay in about (20) fathoms of water. The boxes contained about (17,000,000) pesos (or 7 to 8.5 million dollars). It took ten nights to move the (350) tons of silver to the floor of Caballo Bay.

In the late summer of 1942, when the Japanese had been in control of the Philippines for several months, their occupation currency suddenly began to collapse. Japanese soldiers found that a month's pay wouldn't buy much as a glass of beer. The cause was a mysterious flood of Philippine silver pesos that began turning up in the markets of Manila.

Some how the silver was reaching even the prisoner-of-war camps. American prisoners were bribing demoralized Japanese guards for food, clothing, and medicine. Next they would start buying freedom! If the source of silver wasn't found soon, it could corrupt the whole structure of Japanese control.

The Japanese were well aware of this concealed secret of the jettisoning of the silver into Caballo Bay. Not long after the Island's surrender on 6th May 1942 the Japanese's decided to start a recovery operation of the sunken treasure, when they could round up divers that had some experience in this type of undertaking.

The Japanese's first choice was to hire eight Filipino divers, and an equal number of pump hands, to recover the silver. The divers had only worked in shallow water of Manila Bay, but they were inexperienced in deep water diving techniques and had absolutely no knowledge of the bends or decompression sickness or as some divers call it (The Caisson Disease). It is a painful condition in which nitrogen gets into the blood stream as a result of rising too quickly from the depths. In some cases the diver dies if not treated quickly, or he may wind up a cripple for life.

A native barge, called a "Casco" was fitted out as a diving platform for the Filipino divers and towed to the area where the silver had been dumped. The "Casco" was a flat-bottom barge about sixty feet long and twelve feet wide and a tapered bow and stern. The diving equipment consisted of a U.S. Navy (MK-V) diving dress and helmet and some obsolete hose. An old United States Navy (MK-111) manual operated dive pump is what supplied air to the helmet. The pump was designed to supply air to a maximum depth of ninety feet. It would not furnish adequate ventilation, for safe diving at deeper depths.

An early Mark V helmet   Early Morse air pump

From the beginning, the inexperience of the Filipino divers courted disaster. Dive operations commenced during the later part of May, and the silver was located almost immediately. The divers experienced headaches and fatigue (both symptoms of carbon dioxide excess). Shortly after surfacing, one of the divers was stricken with a painful case of the bends. Lacking the proper knowledge for the bends treatment, the diver was given a vigorous massage. The pain disappeared in a few hours, and the diver returned to work.

Several days passed, and the divers gradually increased their time on the bottom. A few boxes of silver were raised with a long wire strap with an old hand winch mounted on the "Casco". One evening, after a long dive, two of the divers were stricken with serious bends symptoms, and both lost consciousness shortly after surfacing. The previously successful massage treatment was initiated immediately, but was ineffective, for obvious reasons. Both of the divers died in agony during the night.

Terrified by the unexplainable death of their comrades, the remaining divers, with one exception, refused to continue diving. Tempted by the offer of a sizable bonus an increase in pay, one Filipino diver decided to try another method. He reasoned that the bends had been caused by lack of air to the dive suit, and decided to make a dive using the Morse shallow water helmet. This helmet is made of spun copper and it sits on the shoulders of a diver like a diving bell. Air is fed through a gooseneck fitting on top of the helmet and exhaust at shoulder level. The diver made several successful dives using the Morse helmet, and the other divers were about to resume diving when tragedy struck again! The Filipinos were not familiar with the safety precaution of passing the air hose under the divers arm to prevent the helmet from accidentally being pulled off the divers head. When the dive tender pulled the helmet to the surface, no diver was in it. The remaining divers were too frightened by the third death that no amount of urging or promised rewards could convince them to continue diving. The Filipinos had salvaged 18 boxes of silver worth about one hundred thousand pesos.

When Corregidor surrendered 6th May 1942, the Navy divers who had helped in the disposing of the silver were among those taken prisoner. As one of these Navy divers recalled "they took us first to Manila, where they paraded us up and down in the streets for a whole day before we ended up in Bilibid prison, from there by train to Cabanatuan Prison camp and some to another prison camp three days' journey from where we were."

In the latter part of June, the Japanese ordered six prisoners, all U.S. Navy divers from the U.S.S. Pigeon (ASR-6), had to report to the Japanese headquarters in Manila. The six men that were chosen were BM1c Virgil L. Sauers (Jughead) also the senior diver of the group also BM1c Phillip L. Mann (Slim), GM1c George W. McCullough, BM2c Wallace A. Barton (Punchy), CM3c Charles S. Giglio and BM2c Morris Solomon (Moe). The divers were told that the Japanese knew they were divers, and they were being sent to Manila to conduct dive operations. It would have been futile for them to protest and all felt that they would have a better chance to survive and possibly escape in the Manila area.

On the train from Cabanatuna to Manila the captives were well treated. Their captors gave them pork sandwiches and cigarettes. Once they reached Manila, they were escorted to a building near the docks. The six divers were taken to the diving barge "Sasco" on the Pasig River. Then they were told they would dive for boxes on the bottom of the channel. It was soon apparent that they knew about the sunken silver.

After a quick look at the unsafe equipment, BM1c Virgil Sauers, the senior diver, decided to experiment using the Morse Shallow Water Helmet with the (MK-111) hand pump to see if diving could be made relatively safe and a method could be devised to accomplish the dives. The safe depth limit for a Morse hat as the divers call it, is (36 feet or 6 fathoms).

A Morse Shallow Water Helmet

After convincing their captors they needed to find safer equipment, several of the divers got permission to scrounge around the bombed out skeleton of the Dewey Dry Dock in Mariveles Harbor. The trip was made in a Japanese fishing boat. After searching the area they found some diving gear that had been left behind by the U.S.S. Canopus (AS-9). Also retrieved were some newer dive hoses, dive underwear, and non-return valves. The next week or so the divers went to work overhauling the diving equipment and making plans for the dive operation. It was evident by this time, through their contact with the Filipinos, the silver was the object of salvage, and they also knew of the three Filipino dive fatalities.

8th July, the United States diver BM1c Sauers made the first dive. Even with the Filipino pump hands exerting maximum effort to turn the pump handles rapidly, the air supply was barely enough to keep the water from rising above his chin. With each inhalation the water rose to a point just below his month. This of course, meant that should he bend over at any time during the dive, the water would rise over his head.

On BM1c Sauers first dive at the end of the descending line at a depth of (20) fathoms (or 120 feet), he saw boxes stacked one upon the other in a huge pile, with the lower boxes partially buried in the soft silt. He connected a lift wire to one of the boxes and then signaled on his lifeline and air hose to be brought up. An added danger to the operation was absence of decompression tables. Relying on memory, it was decided to decompress for 5 minutes at twenty feet and seven minutes at ten feet. When Sauers reached the surface and the box of silver was raised. The Japanese captain gave Sauers a bottle of Scotch Whiskey for his efforts. Three boxes of silver were raised on the first day.

At the time the first six divers reported to the diving platform there were 3 divers left at the prison camp because of sickness. The three U.S. divers were from the U.S.S. Canopus (AS-9). On 3rd August, the three divers being well enough to go back to diving arrived at the operation on the "Casco". All nine Navy divers names, furnished to the captors by their diving officer. Who later died aboard a prison (death) ship, on it's way to Japan. The new divers were TM1c Robert C. Sheats and he is also an author of a great book "One Man's War" Diving as a guest of the Emperor. TM1c Sheats stayed in the Navy and retired after 31 years, with the rate of Master Chief and Master diver. Also a member of the three is BM1c George J. Chopchick and CM1c Holger Hans Anderson. TM1c Robert C. Sheats brought with him a manual with its antiquated decompression tables. Before R.C. Sheats, G.J.Chopchick and H.H. Anderson left the prison camp the three were told by the commanding officer of the Canopus AS-9 Lt Cdr Frank Davis, a fellow prisoner, "You know what they are really after don't let them get it".

Lt Cdr. Frank Alfred Davis carried on the fighting tradition and valor of his command while interned at the infamous prisoner-of-war camp at Cabanatuna on Luzon Island in the Philippines. Where he built a powerful underground organization to obtain food, medicines and communications of all kinds. He volunteered for command of a firewood detail, and despite the constant surveillance of the Japanese guards, succeeded in smuggling into camp tremendous amounts of food and other necessities to his fellow prisoners. His great personal valor and grave concern for others at a risk to his own life contributed to the welfare and morale of all prisoners on Luzon and saved countless lives before he died 14th December 1944, in the Cabanatuna prison camp. Lt Cdr. Davis received the Navy Cross, for his intrepid fight on the U.S.S. Canopus and the U.S.S. Pigeon (ASR-6) and was posthumously awarded the Legion of Merit for his courageous and dedicated service to his fellow prisoners.

The divers held a meeting in the hold of their living barge and decided that their best course was to appear to cooperate with the salvage master in charge of the operation while doing as much as they could to prevent or delay the silver recovery. Their plan was to bring up boxes on some of the dives and on other dives to tell the Japanese Salvage Master, that they were unable to locate the boxes. Diver CM3c Charles S. Giglio was too inexperienced to engage in the hazardous diving involved, so he was given the task of cook and keeper of the living spaces, for which by records he did an outstanding job.

"It must be remembered that the sea is a great breeder of friendship. Two men who have known each other for TWENTY YEARS find that TWENTY DAYS at sea bring them nearer than ever they were before, or else estrange them." By Gilbert Parker

The boxes of silver were scattered over a wide area. Nearly three thousand boxes had been dumped, but after the cross bearings had been taken, the barges were allowed to drift during the time necessary to off-load. In some areas the boxes were in high piles, in others they were widely scattered. The divers found that, although being in the salt water for only a few months, some of the boxes were beginning to deteriorate. With a moderate amount of effort and with the help of a marlinspike, they could break open the ends of the boxes rather quickly. This presented a great time for sabotage of the silver. For the divers, they quickly agreed that by opening the boxes they would impede the salvage effort greatly. The diver GM1c McCullough smuggled a marlinspike to the bottom, and they used it to break open the boxes when their schedule didn't call for recovery.

At the beginning of the operation the divers smuggled up small amounts of silver pesos in their tennis shoes and under their dive underwear. The silver was then hidden on the dive barge and some divers made up other ways to bring up the silver with them, such as making bags from dungaree pant legs. One of the divers brought with him an old, hard rubber facemask he had used before the war. With the aid of this antiquated mask, makeshift bags for silver, and with the aid of an old gas mask they devised a method of diving to be able to take a significant amount of silver to the beach.

Throughout this recovery process the divers invented all kinds of ways to hide the silver they would bring up from the bottom. The silver was then taken to the beach where the silver was exchanged for food and supplies. The next step in this recovery operation the Japanese announced to the United States divers that they are going to be assisted in the salvage operation by a group of Moro divers. The Moro's are from the Island of Mindanao, and had experience in deep diving for Pearls in the Sulu Archipelago. The United States divers ask very carefully about their dive experience and ability. They said that most of their group had dived to a depth of fifty meters (or a hundred and fifty feet) and that they knew the principles of decompression. So now we have two groups on the dive operation. It was quickly evidenced that their presence on the operation was influenced by high pay offered for their services.

The United States divers that had operated in the Philippines for a time before the war were well aware of the dislike the Moro's had for the Spanish, the northern Filipinos, the Americans and any other group that was against the Muslim tribes of the Southern Islands of the Philippines, there are about (870) islands in all. The dislike for the Americans goes back to about 1913, and this problem still exists today. The Sulu Archipelago, reaches almost to the northern part of Borneo. So this dislike for the Americans would be on the minds of the United States divers, making the diving operation more unconformable for the Americans. They had enough hardships to put up with without this unpleasant problem. Records show that the dislike did not show up at the diving platform or on the beach. The documented history of the Moro people and their fight for freedom is very interesting.

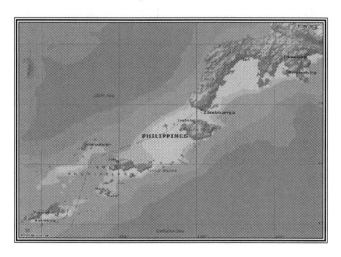

The Sulu Archipelago is from the South tip of Mindanao Island South
and is the home of the Moro people.

The Moro's dive equipment consisted of a British Seibe-Gorman diving
dress and helmet. Air was supplied to the helmet by a three-cylinder
single acting hand pump. Its capacity was larger than the one that the
United States divers were using.

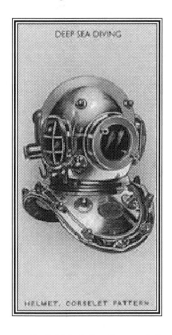

A copy of a British Seibe-Gorman helment

29th September, during typical rough weather preceding the approach of a Typhoon, the diving area operation was shut down as the typhoon approached. The United States divers were taken aboard one of the fishing boats for transportation to Manila. For some reason, not clear to the United States divers, the Moro dive boat was also taken in tow for the trip across the bay. Some place in the trip a United States diver noticed that the towing bridle on the Moro dive boat had slipped, and she was taking on water over her bow. The United States divers, with some difficulties were able to lengthen the line to the bridle of the Moro boat, causing the boat to swamp and then turn over and all the Moro dive equipment was dumped in the bay.

One of the United States divers notified a member of the Japanese crew of the problem. They began flashing signals to the lead fishing boat, and then both boats reversed course and headed back for Corregidor. On the return trip they came upon the overturned dive boat, which they took in tow and the next two or more hours were spent towing the overturned craft back to Corregidor. After arriving back at Corregidor the overturned boat was secured to the dock and the following day a large dock crane lifted the dive boat and placed it on the dock. The Japanese talked together on the dock about the boat and decided that no one person was responsible for the mishap and blamed the swamping to poor seamanship.

The Moro's obtained enough dive equipment in less than a month to resume diving for the silver. To everyone's surprise on 7th November 1942 all diving was discontinued. It was believed that the clearing of all wrecks that lay sunken in Manila Bay was more important than the recovery of the silver. So all divers were put to work diving on the wrecks for salvage throughout the entire Manila Bay. This was done with much danger and difficult conditions until February of 1943. In February the Japanese halted all work on salvage and silver recovery. The recovery of silver was at (approximately sixteen million peso). Only about (one eighth) had been recovered. The United States divers had recovered a total of (ninety-seven boxes,) the Moro's a total of (two hundred and fifty-seven boxes) and the Filipino divers a total of (eighteen boxes), which is a total of slightly over (two million pesos).

This part of the silver recovery is over for all the United States divers, the Moro's and the Filipino divers. The Navy divers were sent back to Cabanatuna prison camp and from there some were sent to Japan by ship to work as slave labor in mines and others remained in prison camps on central Luzon till the end of World War 11. All Navy divers and all other prisoners that survived the war were liberated from Cabanatuna prison camp in September 1945 except Navy diver BM1c George J. Chopchick, he died on a hell ship on the way to Japan in 1944.

The nine divers completed their part in the silver recovery operation, sabotaging, delaying and bringing up the silver to the surface. Smuggling the undetected silver they brought up in their make shift bags and then taking it to the beach for food and medicine. This was an outstanding and dangerous undertaking. These nine divers should be written up as some of the great Navy divers of their time. During their capture they showed outstanding core values of the Navy ("Honor, Courage, Commitment). The Navy motto is also shown in their action and that is ("Non Sibi Sed Patriae") (Not for self, but for Country) which makes this group of Navy divers outstanding Sailors and United States Navy Heroes.

(The divers and their ships)

U.S.S. Pigeon ASR-6
(Minesweeper)
Divers
BM1c V.L. Sauers (Jughead) USN (Senior Diver)
BM1c Phillip L. Mann (Slim) USN
GM1c George W. McCullough USN
Bm2c Wallace A. Barton (punchy) USN
CM3c Charles S. Giglio USN
BM2c Morris Solomon (Moe) USN
BM1c George J. Chopchick USN

U.S.S. Canopus AS-9
(Submarine Tender)
CM1c Holger Hans Anderson USN

TMMC Robert C. Sheats USN (Enlisted July 1935)
2nd Class Diver 1937
1st Class Diver 1939
Master Diver 1958
Retired 1966 as a Master Chief with 31 Years Service
He is an author of
"One Man's War" diving as a guest of the Emperor.

At far left is master diver TMMC Sheats

"A Nation Without Heroes Is Nothing" by (Robert Clements).

" There is no dilemma compared with that of the deep-sea diver who hears the message from the ship above, " come up at once. We are sinking". By (Robert Cooper)

The weight of a Navy divers dry suit, a Mark V can exceed (200) pounds. Just the brass helmet and breastplate weigh (60) pounds.
This dry suit stayed active till 1970, when Scuba gear phased out surface supplied air to dry suits.

Note:

Navy divers are a funny bunch of people, for those who have never met a Navy diver. The Navy diver is legendary, he has fought innumerable sharks, giant squids, engage in an activity for amusement with mermaids, sea snakes have been know to die after biting a Navy diver. If that is hard to believe, just ask a Navy diver. He will verify every word. (Anonymous)

Note:

The Navy diver is not a fighting man, but a salvage expert. If it is lost underwater, he finds it. If it's sunk, he brings it up. If it's in the way, he moves it. If he's lucky, he will die young, (200) feet beneath the waves, for that is the closest a Navy diver will ever get to be in hero status. (Anonymous)

From February of 1943, all remaining boxes and sabotaged loose silver were left resting in the soft silt, undisturbed in Caballo Bay for a couple of years till June of 1945. Leaving about (13,000,000) million pesos to be salvaged.

Silver found by the U.S. Army troops of Company C, 1st Battalion, 130th Regiment, of the 33rd Infantry Division

At this point in the story, the Army discovery of silver should be of interest to anyone that has served in the Army in the Philippines at this point and time. While on patrol outside of Manila on 21st February 1945, Pfc Lou Zerillo, Company C, 1st Battalion, 130th Infantry Regiment, and 33rd Division, with other men of his company, while Pfc Zerillo was crouching in the dirt near Rosario (Our Lady of the most Rosary) a city facing Manila Bay in the province of Cavite. While in this crouching position, with the butt of his weapon uncovered what he first though it was a bottle cap. Looking more closely, he discovered it was a silver coin. Then he spotted another and another. Zerillo stuffed his front pockets with the coins and later an ammunition box as well. Although the division history later recorded that it was artillery round that unearthed the cache of pesos buried near Rosario, Pfc Zerillo remained adamant that he found the coins, saying, "It just isn't so. There are others who were with me that would verify that!" At the time of the discovery, Pfc Zerillo's Company Commander, Captain Patrick Kelly, told the members of Zerillo Patrol "It's now late in the afternoon, and since the Japanese night patrols have a nasty habit of slipping into this sector, I don't want to put a guard on it. We don't want to start a gold rush and get somebody killed just keep this find to yourself!"

Early the next morning Captain Kelly and his patrol went back. As they began unearthing bags of coins, other bags were uncovered, and they soon realized that they had really hit the jackpot. "I watched from above with field glasses and saw Filipinos going over the ground where the pesos were found, said Pfc Zerillo". We fired mortars to scare them off, but I believe they went back in the night and took some more of the pesos. "Besides pesos, I learned later there were United States dollars, gold and Chinese currency." Also laying around were coin wrappers from the Baguio branch of the bank of Formosa, the bank of the Philippines and the National bank of China. It was obvious the rolls of coins were part of the Philippine treasury that had not been dumped into Caballo Bay, but had remained behind in Manila Vaults.

There are conflicting accounts of the value of the coins the soldiers uncovered. Coins recovered by company C, for example, the recovery could be a half a million dollars? Pfc Zerillo disagreed. "I think there was much more. I saw six to ten three-quarter ton weapon carriers with nearly a dozen Filipinos working two full days to move them away from there. Plus there had to be more than what went out in weapon carriers and if you include what was taken by GI's and Filipinos".

While Pfc Zerillo did not credit his discovery of the sliver to artillery rounds, Joe Kutys, who was serving as a company C platoon leader, believed artillery action could have been responsible for the silver surfacing-especially since many of the coins appeared to be fused together, as if from extreme heat.

Another eyewitness Henry Van Westrop, who served as a combat photographer for the 33rd Division, remembered: "What I saw and photographed was the ditch alongside of the road a couple hundred feet long and full of silver pesos. A lot of it was fused together, perhaps from an artillery round, and yet many of the coins looked in new condition."

Another possible reason for the dark color of the silver coins is the action of the salt water on silver. After silver has been in salt water for a time, it will tarnish the coin to a very dark gray. The cache discovered near Rosario could have been a combination of silver recovered from Caballo Bay and the coins that had been left in the bank vaults by retreating Americans. When the Navy divers first learned of the find in 1996, they believed much of the cache discovered near Rosario could have been silver they had recovered from Caballo Bay.

Colonel Arthur Collins was regimental commander of the 130th Infantry. He called Major J.B. Faulconer, regimental operations officer, on the field phone shortly after the coins were discovered near Rosario. "Why are these troops massing instead of dispersing? He demanded. "They are vulnerable as hell to enemy fire!" When Faulconer communicated the reason to the colonel, the order came back: "Retrieve all of it!"

Lieutenant Bernard Donahoe of the division's Combat Intelligence Center (CIC) was hastily summoned from headquarters to assume responsibility for collection and safe removal of the silver before it disappeared. Before trucks left the company area, Collins demanded a receipt for every last peso. Under heavy guard, the money was taken to I Corps Headquarters and turned over to the corps finance officer. Despite efforts to keep souvenir hunters at bay, many 130th Infantry Regiment veterans still possess some of the pesos.

The silver found near Rosario was not the only cache that the American soldiers turned up. A few days after the find by Zerillo's company, 33rd Division artillerymen unearthed ($70,000) more in pesos while digging a new position for their guns.

That ends the first part of our story with millions of silver pesos still at the bottom of Caballo Bay.

From February 1943 to June 1945, the millions of silver pesos wait in their watery grave. Waiting for the start of a new program to recover the silver pesos from Caballo Bay.

The new program of recovering the remaining silver pesos is assigned to two Navy ships equipped with the proper gear, and Navy and Army personnel and Navy and Army divers. The Army personnel handled the radio communications to the divers and other tasks when needed.

The two Navy ships of the Aloe class steel hull net tenders the U.S.S. Teak (AN 35) with Lt. Byron Pierce Hollett USN/R commanding and the U.S.S. Elder (AN 20) with Lt. Joseph C. Patterson USN/R commanding and their crews and the Army personnel came under the command of (Seventh Fleet, Ship Salvage, Fire Fighting and Rescue Group) which was under (Chief of Navy Salvage Operations) and in command was Commodore William Aloysius Sullivan USN and his assistant was Commander W.L. Marshall USN.

The two ships that are assigned to the task are somewhat different than what your normal Navy ship looks like. These funny looking ships with horns that protrude out from the Port and Starboard side of the bow were classified as net tenders. Some made of wood and some made of steel. The next few paragraphs will describe the net tender and her duties during World War two and for a time after the war.

The ship appeared to look like there was a flaw in her design. From the stern they looked like a small class working ship. From the side view is where the small ship took on a different concept of what a standard side view of a ship looks like. Out from the Port and Starboard side of the bow protruded two large horns, they were used as stationary booms for which wire cable or line could be run over the ends that had held steel rollers so the wire or line can run free when lifting and lowering heavy objects. The horns were designed into the hull as a part of the ship, which made for a lot of comments that didn't go over too well with the crews of the small ship. The real purpose of the design of the ship was for the setting and the repairing of nets. The nets were laid across the entrance to harbors, to protect the ships at anchor within the harbor area. The Navy's classification of these very versatile ships is (AN) meaning auxiliary net tenders. Although that was the primary function for these horned ships, some made of wood and others made of steel and not all the same in length, these little ships worked at a variety of many different tasks.

At times a tug, net tender, small cargo ship, repair ship, and salvage ship. A lot of their important work completed while in commission, got very little recognition if any.

Net Tender Descriptions

The Net Tenders were divided into three similar classes of ships. Starting with (AN-1) to (AN-4) which was reclassified to AP's and a length of (458') overall and had no horns.

(AN-1)

(AN-5) was reclassified as (MCS-5) with an overall length of (353') and no horns.

(AN-5)

(AN-6) to (AN-37) the ALOE class had steel hulls and had an overall length of (163'2") and with horns.

ALOE class

The (AN-3) to (AN6 AILANTHUS class had a wooden hull and an overall length of (194'7") and with horns. Also in the same class (AN-70) to (AN-72) where converted to aux tugs (AN-73) to (AN-77) where given to the United Kingdom (as lend lease).

AILANTHUS class

The (AN-78) to (AN-92) CAHOES class with steel hulls and had an overall length of (168'6").

CAHOES class

Now visualize a sailor that has been to sea for some time and served on first line ships of the United States Navy. An a sailor just out of boot camp, with their orders in hand walking down to the end of the pier to their new command. When they check their orders and fine that the hull number matches this thing tied up at the end of the pier, is a small ship with horns, which would leave anyone in shock. There is disbelief that they were ordered to this ship, that by the looks of it could not survive in open sea.

(To the unbelievers the horned Navy, not only survived the open seas but numerous typhoons and all kinds of weather and was sent all over the world to do her thing).

For the sailors that served on this type of ship they all came home a better sailor and with great respect for his ship with horns.

The tenders worked in Great Britain, France, North Africa, Sicily, Newfoundland, Along the East coast of the United States, The Caribbean, Central America, Gulf of Mexico, West coast of the United States, Alaska, Central Pacific, South Pacific, Western pacific, Philippines, Korea, Japan and Viet Nam.

Note:

A short history of one such net tender to show typical work that was accomplished in World War 11 and after the war by this class of ship. This story of one net tender, will give an outline of jobs that most net tenders performed. The story of two net tenders in the recovery of the silver pesos will start at the end of this short story on the U.S.S. Silverbell (AN-51).

<u>The U.S.S. Silverbell (AN-51) story starts at the Pollock-Stockton Shipbuilding Company, Stockton, California.</u>

U.S.S. Silverbell (AN-51)

The U.S.S. Silverbell (YN-70) her keel laid on 7th November 1942 and launched on 19th June 1943, and sponsored by Mrs. Henry Ohm.

Reclassified as (AN-51), 20 January 1944. She is an Ailanthus-class net laying ship with a displacement of 1,275 tons. Ailanthus class is of wooden construction with a length of (194 ft 6in) (59.28m) a beam of (34ft 7in) (10.54m) and a draft of (11ft 8in). Her propulsion is diesel electric, 2,500hp with a speed of 12 knots (22km/h). A complement on most net tenders is (57) Officers and enlisted men.

All net tenders are named after trees. The U.S.S. Silverbell name comes from the (halesia mouticola) silverbell tree. Which are found in the United States in and around the Great Smoky Mountains Park in North Carolina.

16th February
1400: The U.S.S. Silverbell (AN-51) was placed in commission. (Lt. Cdr). F.H. Adams USN/R was the commissioning officer. (Lt.) H.N. Berg USN/R was her new commanding officer. Hoisted the Union Jack and Ensign and broke out the commission pennant. The time was started, the watch set with all hands at quarters at Pullock-Stockton Shipbuilding Company, Stockton California.

16th February to April 29th, this period was spent in preparing ship for sea. Sea trials, checking equipment and training ship's personnel at work and general quarters. Taking on supplies, water and fuel etc. Making recommend repairs, dry dock time, etc. Then on,

22nd February
1015: Underway to San Francisco, California, from Stockton, California.
1655: Moored to Union dock at 17th street, San Francisco.
1857: Underway, for pier (56) in San Francisco, California.
1937: Moored to pier (56), San Francisco, California.

23rd February
0915: Underway, started trial runs.
1250: Anchored off Angel Island, in San Francisco bay.
1301: Underway for Moore's ship and dry-dock Company in Oakland, California.
1403: Moored at pier (7), Moore's ship and dry dock Company.

25th February
0940: Underway, shifting berthing.
0951: Moored to pier (6), Moore's dry dock.
1320: Underway for dry dock number (1), at Moore's dry dock.
1351: Resting on keel blocks in dry dock number (1) for repairs.

27th February
1530: Ship became floating free of keel blocks after repairs.
1542: Underway for Tiburon, California floating dry-dock at training center.
1704: Entered floating dry dock (ARD-16).
1830: Resting on keel blocks for more repairs.

15th March
0821: Ship became floating free of keel blocks after repairs.
0858: Moored to net depot at Tiburon, California.
1009: Underway to enter (ARD-18).
1028: Entered (ARD-18).
1155: Resting on keel blocks no enter in log for being in (ARD-18).

17th March to 18th March no entry in log of leaving (ARD-18) for North Pier (C-2) at Treasure Island, California.

18th March
0000-0400: Moored to North Pier (C-2) at Treasure Island, California.
1102: Underway
1227: Moored to pier (42) of Standard Oil Co.
1524: Underway for Treasure Island, California Section base.
1548: Moored to North pier (C-2) at Treasure Island, California.

19th March
0801: Underway for Mare Island, California
1029: Moored to pier (35) Mare Island, California to take on ammunition.
1118: Underway from pier (35), taken on ammunition completed.

1325: Moored to U.S.S. Tacoma (CL-20) at pier (C-6) Treasure Island, California section base.

20ᵗʰ March
1603: Underway from alongside the U.S.S. Tacoma (CL-20).
1612: Moored to North pier (C-2), Treasure Island, California.

29ᵗʰ March
1316: Underway in San Francisco Bay, California for pier (33) to reduce the ships magnetism.
1345: Moored to pier (33).
1855: Underway to Treasure Island, California.
1937: Moored to starboard side of U.S.S. Saunter (AM 295), pier (C-2), Treasure Island, San Francisco, California

30ᵗʰ March
0730: Underway from North pier berth (C-2) section base Treasure Island, San Francisco, California.
1022: Moored to outer pier (33) San Francisco, California.
1032: Underway, from pier (33).
1048: Passed under Oakland Bay Bridge.
1516: Passed under Oakland Bay Bridge.
1645: Passed through Golden Gate anti-submarine nets.
1655: Passed under Golden Gate Bridge for Sane Diego, California.

Note:
 The ships log has no explanation why from pier (33) it took 16 minutes to get to the Oakland Bay Bridge and 5 hours and 8 minutes to pass under the bridge. Then 1 hour and 29 minutes to get from the bridge to the net gate of the net line that protects San Francisco Bay.

1ˢᵗ April
0000-0400 watch Steaming as before.
1520: Passed San Diego, California bay entrances buoy (1-A).
1623: Moored to North pier at sound school dock San Diego, California.

1st April to 27th April was on shakedown and all kinds of training, from fire fighting, gunnery, general quarters, damage control, man overboard, maintaining and cleaning ship etc. preparing the ship for sea duty. All training finished on the 26th of April.

27th April
1018: Underway for San Francisco, Cailfornia.

29th April
1151: Passed under the Golden Gate Bridge.
1330: Moored alongside U.S.S. Spicewood (AN 53) at north pier (C-6) Treasure Island, California.

1st May
0738: U.S.S. Spicewood (AN53), Underway from alongside.
1312: Underway to Naval Net Depot, Tiburon, California.
1355: Moored to south dock Naval Net Depot, Tiburon, California.
1448: Underway.
1709: Anchored off floating dry dock training center, Tiburon, California.
2215: Underway.
2248: Moored to lighter (YRD-M2) off floating dry dock.
Note: (YRD-M2) is a floating dry dock workshop (machinery). (YRD's) do not have engine rooms. (ABSD-2) Section (20A) is an advanced base sectional dry dock). All ships with a SS before their name are Merchant Marine ships with Navy gun crews.

2nd May
Moored to (YRD-M20), (YRD-M2) Secured to (ABSD-2) Section (20A) in turn secured to tug SS Sabine Pass, anchored off floating dry dock at training center, Tiburon, California. Other ships present of convoy (PW 2393).
0600: Underway still tied to (YRD-M2).
0833: Passed under Golden Gate Bridge in heavy fog.
0841: Cast off (YRD-M2).
1332: Passed San Francisco main channel buoy.

3rd May

0645: Fog lifted, in company with SS Sabine Pass and SS Burnt Island and their tows.

0912: Steaming various courses and speeds while searching for remainder of convoy (PW2393).

1130: SS Sand Key and tow joined the group.

1735: Spotted flashing light on horizon.

1738: Ship identified as U.S.S. Albired (AK90) with convoy (OTC) (Officer-in-Tactical Command) on board and with the remainder of the convoy.

A picture of one section of the dry-dock (256) feet long and (80) feet wide. Each SS tug and the U.S.S. Albired (AK90)
had a section in tow pulse a barge. Making each vessel with two tows.

2148: Resumed position with SS Sand Key, SS Sabine Pass and SS Burnt Island.

6th May, Steaming in company with ships of convoy (PW2393).

Also accompanying the convoy was a Navy tug, the U.S.S. Shahaka (YT 368). Small tug was held in reserve in case any of the SS tugs broke down. Also steaming free of a tow was the U.S.S. Silverbell AN51, also in reserve in case of a break down.

6th May

0640: Standing by to assist SS Sombrero, no help needed.

7th May, Steaming in company with ships of convoy (PW 2393).
0727: Standing by to assist (YT368). No help needed. (YT 368) yard tug.

9th May, steaming in company with ships of convoy (PW2393).
1205: Received message to assist (YT368), reported damage to hull when she attempted to come alongside a dry-dock section. An underwater steel protrusion on the dry-dock section punctured the hull and seawater was pouring in.
1235: The U.S.S. Silverbell (AN-51) alongside (YT368). Men went aboard with a Handy Billy to pump out flooded spaces. It was soon become apparent that the small tug was doomed and was time to abandon ship.
1253: Commanding Officer of (YT368), gave orders to abandon ship. A rope cargo net was put over the side of the U.S.S. Silverbell (AN-51) for the, members of the tug to swiftly come aboard. The only casualty in the rescue was the tugs pet parrot, which was crushed between the two ships.
1312: (YT368) Sank beneath the surface, the U.S. flag on her stern was the last to disappear beneath the waves.
1325: Transferred crew of (YT368) to U.S.S. Albired (AK90).

17th May, Steaming in company with ships of convoy (PW2393).
1056: Sounded general quarters to go alongside U.S.S. Albired (AK90) for orders.
1110: Received orders from convoy Commodore on U.S.S. Albired (AK90) to proceed to SS Sombrero Key and instruct that vessel's master was authorized to give orders to Navy gun crew.
1134: Passed close aboard the SS Sombrero Key and instructed its master as directed by the convoy Commodore. (Captain Berg and the captain of the SS tug communicated by megaphones. Captain Berg had learned that the Navy gun crew had disobeyed orders from the tugs Captain. Captain Berg by orders of the Commodore said to the Navy gun crew " to disobey the order of a ship's Captain is mutinous and, has naval officer, I order you to obey". Out come of what happen to the Navy gun over the disobeying of a direct order was never known by the U.S.S. Silverbells (AN-51) crew.

1210: Close aboard the SS Paint Judith. No help needed.

22nd May, Steaming as before in Convoy (PW2393).

1555: Davy Jones came aboard to serve subpoenas and to initiate all pollywogs into the solemn mysteries of the ancient order of the deep.

Note:

It is well known that ceremonies took place long ago when the ship crossed the line. Early ceremonies were rough and to a great extent supposed to try the crew to determine whether or not the novices on their first cruise could endure the hardships of life at sea. The custom then, as at present, is primarily a crew's party.

The Vikings were reported at an early date to carry out these ceremonies on crossing the certain parallels. It is highly probable that the present day ceremony was passed on to the Anglo-Saxon's, and Norman's from the Vikings. As at earlier times, ceremonies of propitiation are carried on to appease Neptune, the mythological god of the seas. Those who have crossed the line, the equator, are called shellbacks. The sons of Neptune compose the cast for the present day ceremonies.

The certificate in which testifies that "in Latitude 00-00 and Longitude XX-XX. Usually addressed to all Mermaids, Sea Serpents, Whales, Sharks, Porpoises, Dolphins, Skates, Eels, Suckers, Lobsters, Crabs, Pollywogs and all living things of the sea. Insert (sailors name) has been found worthy to be numbered as one of our trust shellback, has been gathered to our fold and duly initiated into the solemn mysteries of the ancient order of the deep."

Members of Neptunus Rex's party include Davy Jones, Neptune's first assistant, Her Highness Amphitrite, the Royal Scribe, the Royal Doctor, the Royal Dentist, the Royal Baby, the Royal Navigator, the Royal Chaplain, Judges, Attorneys, Barbers and other names that suit the party. The uninitiated are pollywogs or worse, landlubbers.

This is a copy of a subpoena for May 1944. Subpoena from Davy Jones, Clerk of the Court of Neptune, to a Crossing the line Ceremony, 1944.

IN THE ROYAL COURT OF THE REALM OF NEPTUNE
In And For The District Of EQUATORIUS

SUBPOENA

INHABITANTS OF THE REALM OF THE DEEP

VS

Pollywog (name of sailor) U.S. Navy.

You are hereby commanded to appear before the ROYAL COURT
OF THE REALM OF NEPTUNE, in the DISTRICT OF
EQUATORIUS. Because it has been brought to the attention of his
HIGHNESS NEPTUNE REX. Through his trusty SHELLBACKS
that the good ship SILVERBELL AN-51 is about to enter those
waters manned by crew who have not acknowledged the sovereignty
of the RULER OF THE DEEP, has transgressed on his domain and
thereby incurred his Royal displeasure.

THEREFORE be it known to all ye Box Car Tourists, Park Statues,
Cream puffs, Hay Makers, and Politicians that His Most Royal
NEPTUNE REX. Supreme Ruler of all Mermaids, Sharks, Squids,
Crabs, Pollywogs, Eels and other denizens of the deep. Will, with
his Secretary and Royal Court, meet in full session on board the
offending ship U.S.S. Silverbell (AN-51) on 23rd day of May A.D.
1944, to hear your defense on the charges of.

An example of Charges for one sad sailor (pollywog) on board the
U.S.S. Silverbell. (AN-51).

1) Calling bulkheads walls
2) Banging ears with the Boat's
3) Stuffing your gut
4) Always first in the chow line
5) Not knowing the correct terms for items found on board ship
6) Not studying for your next rate

7) Call the head the bathroom

It is therefore ordered and decreed that the above names man present himself before the above Court at the time and place above mentioned or else be condemned to become food for Sharks, Whales, Pollywogs, Frogs, and all other scum of the sea, who will devour your head, body and soul- as a warning to any Landlubbers entering my Domain, disobey this order under my displeasure- INCARNATION IN DAVY JONES' LOCKER!!!!!

BY ORDER OF THE COURT:

Given under my hand this 23rd Day of May 1944.

DAVY JONES, Clerk,
Honorable Pegleg,
Deputy

23rd May Underway as before in convoy (PW2393).
1233: King Neptune and his Royal Party departed the U.S.S. Silverbell (AN-51), having initiated and accepted with due ceremony thirty-seven newly christened shellbacks, into his Royal Domain.

31st May, Steaming in company with ships of convoy (PW2393).
1146: Sighted Olosega Island, of Manua group.

1st June 1944 Steaming in company with ships of convoy (PW2393).
0450: Sighted Pago Pago

4th June, Steaming in company with ships of convoy (PW2393).
0945: Sighted Hoorn Island.

5th June, Steaming in company with ships of convoy (PW2393).

5th June
0100: Crossed the International Date Line.

6th June, Steaming in company with ships of convoy (PW2393).
0920: Passed tow wire to SS Burnt Island.
0925: SS Burnt Island in tow.
1600: SS Burnt Island cast off tow wire.

11th June, Steaming in company with ships in convoy (PW2393).
0653: Sighted Meralav Island.
1625: Sighted Cape Cumberland, Espiritu Santo Island.

19th June, Steaming in company with ships of convoy (PW2393).
0850: Commenced Passing mail to, (ABSD2) section (F), SS Sand Key, (ABSD2) section (E), SS Burnt Island, (ABSD2) section (C), (YRD (H) 2), (ABSD2) section (S), SS Sombrero Key, (YRD (M) 2), (ABSD2) section (A), SS Sabine Pass, (ABSD2) section (B), SS Point Julith.
1135: Completed mail run.

20th June, Steaming in company with ships of convoy (PW2393).
0625: Sighted Cape Cretin, New Guinea.
1050: Sighted Rooke (Umboi) Island
1610: Sighted Long Island.

21st June, Steaming in company with ships of convoy (PW2393).
1655L Sighted Baluan Island.
1745: Sighted Alim Island.
2250: Sighted Johnson Island.

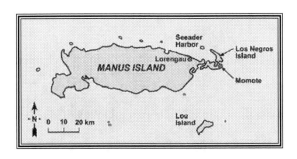

Manus Island, Admiralty Islands

The Admiralty Island was a German protectorate from 1884 to 1914. Seeadler Harbor at Manus Island, Admiralty Islands is named after a German raider the SMS Seeadler (English meaning is Sea Eagle) her Captain was Count Felix Von Lucker. At that time the Islands were called German New Quinea.

SMS Seeadler

June 22nd

1215: With all ships of convoy (PW2393), entered Seeadler Harbor, Manus Island, Admiralty Islands. Having been at sea for (51days). Steaming at an average speed of 6 knots since leaving San Francisco, California.

The six sections of (ABSD-2) and barges reassembled in Seeadler Harbor, Manus Island. Admiralty Islands.

1431: Anchored in berth (235). U.S.S. Tangier (AV8) Seaplane tender is (SOPA).

24th June
Commence work on laying moorings.

26th June
Completed laying moorings.

27th June to 11th July
Working on (A&T) net laying operations. Working under the directions from the U.S.S. Indus (AKN-1) (Cargo ship carrying net cargo for net operation). (A&T Anti torpedo net)

11th July 1944
1115: Moored alongside U.S.S. Cinnamon (AN50)

12th July
0713: Underway from alongside the U.S.S. Cinnamon (AN50). Commence work on nets.

12th of July to the 29th of July: Working on net operations.

29th July
Commenced operation of laying battleship moorings

30th July
Completed laying battleship moorings.

31st July
Anchored near U.S.S Euryale (AS-22) to effect repairs to evaporators. 1325: Moored to U.S.S. Euryale (AS-22) with (S42) moored to portside with (S45) moored outboard of (S42). (For submarines (S42) and (S45) they are renumbered to (SS153 and (SS156)

1st August to 5th August, Moored as before. U.S.S. Whitney (AD4)

(SOPA)
0646 on the 1ˢᵗ of August, The S42 and S45 got underway from alongside.

5ᵗʰ August to 7ᵗʰ August, Worked at laying battleship moorings.

7ᵗʰ of August completed mooring project. U.S.S. Meduse (AR1) is (SOPA)

8ᵗʰ August
Working on channel gate, for (A&T) net line.

11ᵗʰ August
1455: Inspected bottom of ship in light diving outfit. Completed inspection of bottom. Condition satisfactory. U.S.S. Nashville (CL-43) is (SOPA).

12ᵗʰ August
Working on laying and completing telephone cable attached to top of (A&T) net line.

15ᵗʰ August
Laid mooring for berth (317)
1620: Completed operation.

16ᵗʰ August, Anchored in Seedler Harbor, Manus Island. U.S.S. Sagamon (AO-28) is (SOPA).
1320: Underway for the U.S.S. Porcupine (IX126)
1430: Moored to U.S.S. Porcupine (IX126).
1548: Underway from alongside U.S.S Porcupine (IX126).
1630: Anchored in anchorage in Seeadler Harbor, Manus Island. Admiralty Islands.

17ᵗʰ August
1135: U.S.S. Cinnamon (AN50) came alongside.
1310: U.S.S. Cinnamon (AN50) underway from alongside.
1340: Underway for Biak Island, in the Netherlands East Indies, in

company with the U.S.S. Quapaw (AT-110) (a fleet tug).
1410: Passed through harbor net.

18ᵗʰ August, ship underway as before.
0005: Casualty to main propulsion motor rheostat, causing ship to lose power.
0344: U.S.S. Quapaw (AT110) came alongside to pass a towline in order to tow us back to Manus Island, in the Admiralty Islands.
0700: Sighted Manus Island.
1836: Moored alongside U.S.S. Quapaw (AT110) off Lombrum point, Los Negros Island in the Admiralty Islands.

19ᵗʰ August
0000-0400: Moored alongside (YOG19) moored to U.S.S. Quapaw (AT110) at repair dock.
0830: Underway from alongside (YOG19). Proceeding to anchorage.
0932: Anchored in anchorage.
1437: Underway. Proceeding to U.S.S. Cinnamon (AN50).
1526: Moored alongside the U.S.S. Cinnamon.

20ᵗʰ August, Moored alongside the U.S.S. Cinnamon (AN50). U.S.S. Medusa (AR1) (SOPA).
0828: Mr. Mitchell civilian Raytheon engineer came aboard to adjust ships (SO-1) radar equipment.
1254: Underway, from alongside the U.S.S. Cinnamon (AN50) to go alongside the U.S.S. Quapaw (AT110).
1432: Moored alongside the U.S.S. Quapaw (AT110).
1825: Mr. Mitchell left the ship.

21ˢᵗ August, Moored alongside the U.S.S. Quapaw (AT110), Manus Island in Seeadler Harbor, Admiralty Islands. U.S.S. Medusa (AR1) is (SOPA)
1101: Underway from alongside U.S.S. Quapaw (AT110) for Mios Woendi Lagoon at Biak Island in the Padaido Islands.
1256: Passed through Harbor net gate in company with the U.S.S. Quapaw (AT110).

22nd August, Steaming in company with the U.S.S. Quapaw (AT110).
1840: Sighted land, identified as New Guinea coast.

23rd August, Steaming in company with the U.S.S. Quapaw (AT110).

24th August, Steaming in company with the U.S.S. Quapaw (AT110).
0623: Sighted Padaido Island.
1037: Entering Mios Woendi Lagoon, Biak Island in the Padaido Islands in the Netherlands East Indies.
1110: Anchored in Mios Woendi Lagoon, Biak Island.

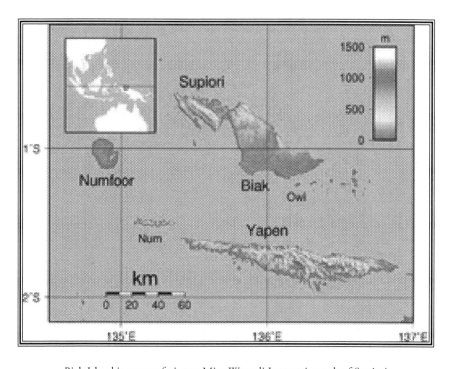

Biak Island is at top of picture Mios Woendi Lagoon is south of Supiori

Map showing an overall view of the area Northwest of New Guinea.

25th August, Moored as before. U.S.S. Tangier (AV8)(SOPA)
1355: Underway for Mios Woendi dock.
1427: Moored to Mios Woendi dock.
1547: Underway, for anchorage.
1613: Anchored in anchorage

26th August, Anchored as before. U.S.S. Tangier (AV8) is (SOPA).
1027: U.S.S. Teaberry (AN34) came alongside.
1536: U.S.S. Teaberry (AN34) underway from alongside.

27,28,29,30 of August, Anchored as before. U.S.S. Tangiers (AV8) is (SOPA)

29th August
Note:
    On the 29th of August, all Navy ship's present in Mios Woendi Lagoon, the commanding officers of all ship's present gave liberty to all personnel that did not have the duty. The liberty was for the Bob Hope's USO show on the beach. Liberty uniform was your clean work uniform. The Navy's was dungarees and white hat. All the other services also a clean work uniform.

The USO show came to Biak Island only a few months after the Island was secured. The area on the Island for the show was an area that had been bombed a lot. So military personnel cleaned up the area, and then made a make shift stage. The setting area was made up by bomb out palm tress and anything that could be made into for sitting.

All personnel for the show is now sited or standing. Then Bob Hope comes out on stage with a standing ovation. He stop's and reviews the audience, the walks to one side of the stage and look's at two standing sailors and motions for them to come on stage. Finally they made it to the stage, and then Bob Hope hands them two swabs and said for them to swab down the stage before they could start the show. With a smile you could see from the Lagoon they swab down the stage. When the job was done Bob Hope ask them to stay on stage with swabs in hand, incase it rained again. To the side of the stage they went with swabs in hand to wait for it rain. After they finished swabbing the stage all military personnel gave then a big ovation. The two sailors that did the swabbing down of the stage will remember the swabbing down forever.

After placing the two sailors on stage, Bob Hope looked down into Officers country. Which is right in front of the stage. Bob saw a lot of empty seats and said to the Officers the show will start when all empty seats in Officers Country are full of standing enlisted personnel. With all seats full, Bob started the show.

The Bob Hope's USO show was made up of the greatest entertainers in the business. For this show it was Bob Hope, Jerry Colona, Francis Langford, Patricia (Patty) Thomas, Jerry Romano, Lanny Ross and Les Brown and his band of renown.

The show was the greatest anyone had seen in a very long time. To top off the show is when Bob Hope chased Patty Thomas around and around the stage trying to unzip her bathing suite. To the disappointment of all personnel he never could catch her. He still gat a standing ovation for trying.

Bob Hope and his troupe will always be our Hero's, for what they did for all troupes all over the world during World War 11 and after.

After the show and while on the beach, the military personnel was introduced to a famous Biak island drink called "Jamade" made by filling a garbage can with warm water, then dumping gallon cans of jam into the warm water, then with a long stick or broom handle. Then stir for a time, till all ingredients are mixed well.

31st August, Anchored as before. U.S.S. Tangiers (AV8) is (SOPA).
0815: Underway for the U.S.S. Indus (AKN-1) (cargo ship)
0827: Moored to the U.S.S. Indus (AKN-1).
1441: Underway, from alongside the U.S.S Indus (AKN-1) to lay two utility moorings.
1506: Work completed laying the two utility moorings. Moored to East utility mooring.

1st September, Moored as before in Mios Woendi lagoon, at Biak Island. U.S.S. Tangiers (AV8) is (SOPA).
0806: Underway, to install five (SONO) buoy moorings.
1420: Completed operations of laying (SONO) buoy moorings.
1440: Anchored in Mios Woendi lagoon, Biak Island.

3rd September, Anchored as before. U.S.S. Tangiers (AV8) is (SOPA).
0917: Underway, for the U.S.S. Orion (AS18).
0933: Moored alongside the U.S.S. Orion (AS18).
1715: Underway from alongside the U.S.S Orion (AS18).
1855: Anchored in Mios Woendi lagoon, Biak Island.

5th September, Anchored as before.
0730: Underway, for A/T net operations.

6th September to 13th September, Worked at A/T net operations.

13th September, Anchored in Mios Woendi lagoon. U.S.S Tangiers (AV8) is (SOPA).
0704: Underway, to lay gate for A.T net line.
1107: Completed installation of net gate at A/T net line.
1132: Anchored in Mios Woendi lagoon anchorage.

14th September, Anchored as before. U.S.S. Tangiers (AV8) is

(SOPA).

1025: Underway, for the U.S.S. Salamonia (AO26).

1110: Moored to the U.S.S. Salamonia (AO26).

1250: Underway, from alongside the U.S.S. Salamonia (AO26) to anchorage in Mios Woendi lagoon.

15th September, Anchored as before. U.S.S. Tangiers (AV8) is (SOPA)

0850: Underway for the U.S.S. Indus (AKN-1).

0859: Moored alongside the U.S.S. Indus (AKN-1).

1539: Underway, from alongside the U.S.S. Indus (AKN-1) for anchorage.

1642: Anchored in Mios Woendi lagoon.

19th September, Anchored as before. U.S.S. Tangiers (AV8) is (SOPA).

0800: Underway, to entrance to (A/T) net line.

1139: Anchored at (A/T) net line.

1244: Underway shifting net entrance gate (400) feet east.

2057: Completed shifting net gate. Anchored in Mios Woendi lagoon anchorage.

20th September, Anchored as before in Mios Woendi lagoon. U.S.S. Phoenix (CL46) is (SOPA)

21st September, Anchored as before. U.S.S. Phoenix (CL46) is (SOPA)

0448: Heavy rain squall. Motor launch swamped.

0625: Motor launch recovered.

1535: Made preparations for getting underway. Net operations completed.

1600: Underway, proceeding to sea, destination, Seeadler Harbor, Manus Island in the Admiralty Islands.

1608: Passed thru net gate.

1610: Took station (600) yards of port beam of U.S.S. Indus (AKN-1).

22nd September, Steaming as before, in company with U.S.S. Indus (AKN-1).

1130: U.S.S. Indus (AKN-1) chose to leave us to meet her time schedules.

1300: Steaming independently for Seeadler Harbor, Manus Island. Admiralty Islands.

23rd September, Steaming independently as before.

24th September, Steaming independently as before.

0510: Sighted Hermit Island.

2017: Passed through net gate into Seeadler Harbor, Manus Island. Admiralty Islands.

2108: Moored alongside the U.S.S Cinnamon (AN50) for anchorage in Seeadler Harbor, Manus Island. Admiralty Islands.

1343: Anchored in Seeadler Harbor, Manus Island. Admiralty Islands.

26th September, Anchored as before. U.S.S. Argonne (AG31) is (SOPA).

0800: Underway to go alongside the U.S.S. Torchwood (AN55).

0827: Moored alongside the U.S.S Torchwood (AN55).

0855: Underway from alongside the U.S.S. Torchwood (AN55) to ship repair dock at Lombrum Point in Seeadler Harbor, Manus Island. Admiralty Islands.

0902: Moored to ship repair dock at Lombrum point in Seeadler Harbor, Manus Island. Admiralty Islands.

0927: (LCI 634) moored alongside. (LCI) is a landing craft infantry)

0932: (LCI 700) moored outboard of (LCI 634).

27th September, Moored as before, with two (LCI's) alongside at Lombrum point in Seeadler Harbor, Manus Island. Admiralty Islands. U.S.S. Argonne (AG31) is (SOPA).

28th September, Moored as before, with two (CLI'S) alongside at Lombrum point, Seeadler Harbor, Manus Island. Admiralty Islands. U.S.S. Argonne (AG31) is (SOPA).

1300: (LCI 1008) and (LCT 720) came alongside the two outboard

(LCI'S 634)&(700) and moored outboard to (LCI 700).
1400: (LCI'S 1171), 727) and (1169) moored outboard to (LCT 720).

29th September, Moored as before to Lombrum point repair dock in Seeadler Harbor. U.S.S. Argonne (AG31) is (SOPA).

Note: No entry log to what happen to (LCI'S) and (LCT) that where moored alongside.

0808: Underway from alongside Lombrum point repair dock to anchorage in Seeadler Harbor, Manus Island, Admiralty Islands.
0922: Anchored in assigned berth in Seeadler Harbor, Manus Island. Admiralty Islands.

30th of September to 2nd October, Anchored in anchorage, in Seeadler Harbor, Manus Island. Admiralty Islands. Shifted anchorage two times to prevent dragging (In heavy storm). U.S.S Argonna (AG31) is (SOPA).

3rd October, Anchored as before in Seeadler Harbor, Manus Island. Admiralty Islands. U.S.S. Argonne (AG31) is (SOPA).
2216: Underway singly, proceeding to (A/S) net gate at entrance to Seeadler Harbor, Manus Island. Admiralty Islands.
2301: Passed through (A/S) net gate, destination Milne Bay, Papua Island. New Guinea.

4th October, Steaming singly, destination Milne Bay, Papua Island. New Guinea.
1643: Sighted Tolokuva Island.

6th October, Steaming singly as before.
0448: Sighted Eleanor shoal light.
0553: Sighted Eve shoal buoy.
1613: Sighted Veale reef buoy.
2046: Sighted Ipoteto island light.

7th October, Steaming singly as before.
Waiting for daylight to enter Raven Channel.
0628: Sighted Teadover reef.
0709: Entered Raven Channel.
0719: Raven Channel light buoys abeam to Port Starboard.
0830: Cleared of Raven Channel.
0842: Sighted Sullivan Patch buoy.
0930: Sighted coast of New Guinea.
1105: Sighted entrance to Milne Bay, Papua Island. New Guinea.
1155: Anchored in Milne bay, Papua Island. New Guinea.
1427: Underway to go alongside the U.S.S Indus (AK-1)
1440: Moored alongside the U.S.S. Indus (AK-1) is (SOPA).

9th October, Moored as before, alongside the U.S.S. Indus (AKN-1), in Gili anchorage Milne Bay, Papua Island. New Guinea.
1252: Underway from alongside the U.S.S. Indus (AKN-1) and proceeding to the SS Rocklea (SS tanker).
1318: Moored to the SS Rocklea to take on fuel.
1515: Fueling completed, underway and proceeding to anchorage in Milne bay.
1523: Anchored in Gili anchorage in Milne bay, Papua Island. New Guinea.

11th October, Anchored as before in Milne bay, Papua Island, New Guinea. U.S.S. Indus (AKN-1) is (SOPA).
1030: Underway steaming singly for Humbolt Bay, Hollandia, Netherlands. New Guinea.
1525: Passed entrance buoy ("B") leaving Milne bay, Papua Island, New Guinea. Steaming singly destination Humbolt Bay, Hollandia, Netherlands. New Guinea.

Note: the log has the ship taking 5 hours to go from the anchorage in Milne Bay, entrance buoy ("B").

12th October, Steaming singly, destination Humbolt Bay, Hollandia, Netherlands. New Guinea.
0415: Sighted Tufi Leads light.

0450: Sighted Ham reef light.

12th October to 15th October, Steaming singly, destination Humbolt Bay, Hollandia, Netherlands. New Guinea.

15th October
0650: Entered Humbolt Bay, Hollandia, Netherlands. New Guinea.

Humbolt Bay, Hollandia, Netherlands. New Guinea.

0800: Moored alongside the U.S.S. Cinnamon (AN50).
1300: Underway from alongside the U.S.S. Cinnamon (AN50). Commenced running degaussing range.
1333: Completed degaussing runs and started swinging ship to compensate compass.
1415: Completed compensation of compass.
1435: Anchored in Humbolt Bay, Hollandia, Netherlands. New Guinea.

16th October
    Anchored in Humbolt Bay, Hollandia, Netherlands. New Guinea. After the main body of ships, left Hollandia for the invasion of the Philippines. Today looking around the bay and out to sea and as far as you can see, is nothing but ships of all kinds. To have seen this armada, it is difficult to put into words the size. Only a person observing this mass of ships can come close to explaining the size.

Note:

On this 16th day of October General Douglas MacArthur and staff left Humblot Bay, Hollandia, Neterlands, New Guinea on his flagship the U.S.S. Nashville (CL43).

The flagship and General MacArthur left Hollandia with a great task force, being one of two task forces. The second task force was leaving Seeadler harbor in the Admiralty Islands, both units to arrive at Leyte Gulf on October 20th. Both units are made up of ships every kind, aircraft carriers, cruisers and destroyers and a massive array; of transports and landing craft. Total number of ships making up the two task forces was 700 ships. Carring 174,000 fighting men. (Making the two units the greatest armada in history). Being a quote from General MacArthur. The two task forces arrived on time on October 20th at Leyte Gulf.

Smaller convoys arrived a few days later in Leyte Gulf. For a time the Gulf was a sea of ships of all kinds.

16th October
0809: Underway to take on fuel from U.S.S. Shimellamy (AOG47).
0836: Moored alongside the U.S.S. Shimellamy (AOG47) to take on fuel.
1024: Underway from alongside the U.S.S. Shimellamy (AOG47) taking on fuel completed.
1107: Anchored in anchorage in Humbolt Bay, Hollandia, Netherlands. New Guinea.

18th October: Anchored as before in Humbolt Bay, Hollandia, Netherlands. New Guinea.
0604: Underway from Humbolt Bay, Hollandia, Netherlands. New Guinea. To join task unit (TG 77.7) convoy.
0728: Joined task unit (TG 77.7) a convoy of (70) ships and took station (#27), (600) yards astern of U.S.S. Caribou (IX-144).

19th October to 24th October, Steaming in convoy (TG 77.7) at station (#27), astern of the U.S.S. Caribou (IX-144).

20th October

General MacArthur arriving in Leyte Gulf, on the U.S.S. Nashville (CL43). The Nashville is lying to about two miles off Red beach. He and his staff with other importation people are then transferred to a small landing craft. The landing craft runs aground just short of Palo Beach (Red Beach). General MacArthur and staff also the Philippine President Sergio Osmena and the Philippine General Carlos R. Romulo. Are aground short of the beach General MacArthur "we will wade ashore". At this point MacArthur wades into history.

There are many stories about the general and staff wading ashore at red beach. There are true stories and there are ones in question. The truth is that he did wade ashore and we know that is true.

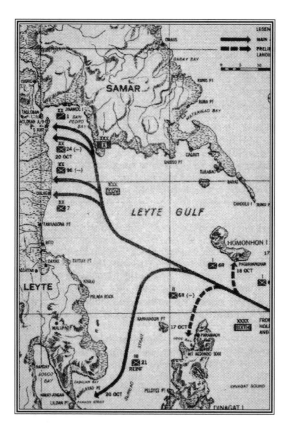

Map of Leyte Gulf, Philippine Islands on October 20th, 1944.

The invasion units coming from Humbolt Bay, Hollandia, Netherlands, New Guinea and Seeadler Harbor, Manus in the Admiralty Island, and arriving on the 20th of October 1944, at Leyte Gulf, Leyte, Philippine Islands. The map show's the invasion route from the (Southerly) corner of the map and moving along a line (Northwesterly). Moving along in a (Northwesterly) direction at different intervals, smaller units branched off to different beaches.

At the NW corner of the map the two northerly arrows and most northerly arrow is <u>WHITE</u> beach, the next arrow South is <u>RED</u> beach where MacArthur and staff waded ashore. The next two arrows to the South are <u>YELLOW</u>, <u>ORANGE</u> and BLUE beaches.

Wading ashore at Red beach in Leyte Gulf on October 20th 1944 is MacArthur, and staff.

24th October
0300: The U.S.S. Silverbell (AN 51) entered Leyte Gulf, Philippine Islands with all (70) units of Task unit (TG 77.7) convoy.
1635: All units anchored in San Pedro Bay, Leyte Gulf, in the Philippine Islands. U.S.S. Wasatch (AGC-9) is (SOPA)

24th October to 27th October Ship at general quarters (75%) of the time.

27th October, Anchored in San Pedro Bay, Leyte Gulf, Leyte, Philippine Islands.

2150: Underway to deliver fire fighting equipment to U.S.S. Cable (ARS19) at scene of fire.

2320: Anchored near the U.S.S. Cable (ARD19) off (RED BEACH).

28th October to 29th October, Anchored and underway from small salvage operations and (at general quarters most of the time). Ship anchored in San Pedro Bay, Leyte, in the Philippine Islands. U.S.S. Wasatch (AGC9) is (SOPA).

30th October, Anchored as before in San Pedro Bay, Leyte Gulf, Philippine Islands. U.S.S. Wasatch (AGC-9) is (SOPA). Typhoon in progress, Starboard engine started to help hold heading while anchored.

0430: Typhoon ended.

0525: PT 495 moored alongside.

0640: PT 495 underway from alongside.

0754: Underway for Tacloban harbor with tow. (No description of tow or how we came to have it in tow).

0924: Anchored in Tacloban harbor. (No entry in ships log to what happened to tow).

1055: Underway from Tacloban harbor to anchorage in San Pedro Bay.

1203: Anchored in San Pedro Bay, Leyte Gulf, Leyte, in the Philippine Islands.

1300: Underway to begin salvage operation. (Description of what type of salvage was not entered in ships log).

1340: Anchored at salvage area.

1615: Salvage operations completed underway to anchorage in San Pedro Bay,Leyte Gulf, Leyte, Philippine Islands.

1718: Anchored in San Pedro Bay. (General quarters most of the day).

31st October, Anchored as before in San Pedro Bay, Leyte Gulf, Leyte, Philippine Islands. U.S.S. Wasatch (AGC-9) is (SOPA).

1016: Underway to Dulag

1300: Anchored off Dulag, Leyte Gulf, Leyte, in the Philippine Islands. In preparatory to pull broached barges off beach.
1624: Underway, from Gulag with barges in tow for Tacloban, Leyte Gulf, Leyte, Philippine Islands.

1754: Ran over shoal. No apparent damage. Put boat in water to sound shoal. Found least depth of shoal to be (12 feet). Buoy of shoal found to be out of position.

1932: Anchored in San Pedro Bay, Leyte Gulf, Leyte, in the Philippine Islands. (In and out of general quarters most of the day).

1ˢ November Anchored as before in San Pedro Bay, Leyte Gulf, Leyte, in the Philippine Islands. U.S.S. Qasatch (AGC-9) is (SOPA).

Note:
    While the ammunition barge was alongside a group of four bogeys singled us out for attention and took us by surprise before general quarters had sounded. The crew had just finished our noon meal when a loud explosion shook the ship. From the explosion water propelled by a near miss covering the superstructure. Then falling to the main deck like a waterfall. If the bomb had hit the ammunition barge, the U.S.S. Silverbell (AN-51) and her entire crew would have been destroyed.

0630: Underway, with pontoon barges in tow.
0825: Anchored off Tacloban, passed pontoon barges to Seabee's.
0852: Underway for Dulag to salvage pontoon barges.
1133: Commenced salvage operations.
1837: Completed salvage operations, underway for <u>WHITE BEACH.</u>
2020: Anchored off <u>WHITE BEACH</u>, San Pedro Bay, Leyte Gulf, Leyte, Philippine Islands. U.S.S. Wasatch (AGC-9) is (SOPA). (Most of the day spent at general quarters).

2ⁿᵈ November, Anchored as before in San Pedro Bay, Leyte Gulf, Leyte, Philippine Islands. U.S.S. Wasatch (AGC-9) is (SOPA).
1020: Underway for Dulag.

1206: Anchored off <u>YELLOW</u> Beach preparatory to pulling pontoon barges off the beach. (General quarters off and on all day).
1933: Proceeding to safe anchorage.
1953: Anchored off Dulag. Ship still at general quarters.
2000: Secured from general quarters.

3rd November, Anchored in San Pedro Bay, Leyte Gulf, Leyte, Philippine Islands.
0500: Underway for Dulag.
0555: Anchored off Dulag, preparatory to pulling barges off beach.
1834: Underway.
1836: Anchored off Dulag.

4th November, Anchored as before in San Pedro Bay, Leyte Gulf, Leyte, Philippine Islands.
0630: Underway with pontoon barges and proceeding to Tacloban.
1120: Anchored off Tacloban, passed barges to Seabee's.
1150: Underway
1310: Moored alongside the U.S.S. Severn (AO61) to take on fresh water.
1403: Underway from alongside the U.S.S. Severn (AO61).
1430: Anchored in San Pedro Bay, Leyte Gulf, Leyte, in the Philippine Islands.
1820: Underway to retrieve (PT526) from the beach.
1900: Anchored off Tinze point.

5th November, Anchored as before off Tinze point, Samar Island. U.S.S. Fremont (LPA44) is (SOPA). (Most of the night and morning spent at general quarters).
0737: Underway to take position to pull (PT526) from beach.
0742: Anchored for pulling (PT526) from beach.
1915: (Secured from general quarters). (PT526) pulled off beach.
1945: (PT526) moored alongside.

6th November, Anchored as before U.S.S. Fremont (LPA44) is (SOPA)
0627: Underway with (PT526) alongside.

0700: (LCM) from boat pool took (PT526) from alongside.

0845: Moored alongside the U.S.S. Indus (AKN-1).

1613: Underway.

1637: Anchored in San Pedro Bay, Leyte. Philippine Islands.

7th November, Anchored as before. U.S.S. Fremont (LPA44) is (SOPA)

0630: Underway to install (SONO) buoys in Leyte Gulf, Leyte, in the Philippine Islands.

1645: Completed (SONO) buoy operation, anchored off Point Desolation, Dinagat Island, Philippine Islands.

8th November, Anchored as before off Point Desolation Dinagat Island, Philippine Islands. The barometer is falling on the (0000 to 0400) watch. Buoy boat moored to bow.

0400: Sounded general quarters to rouse crew to save buoy boat.

1422: Barometer still falling, line to buoy boat parted. Buoy boat last seen afloat and drifting away from ship.

1615: Ship commenced to rolling violently, (50) degrees to Port and Starboard.

1620: Cut anchored loose, underway to ride out storm (Typhoon).

1930: Typhoon reach maximum strength.

9th November, Steaming as before to ride out Typhoon off Leyte Gulf, Philippine Islands.

0200: Typhoon began to quiet down.

0900: Sea almost back to normal, steaming as before

1200-1600 Watch: Steaming various courses to make a count of (SONO) buoys that have been laid.

10th November, Steaming as before, between Dinagat Island and Homonhon Islands in Leyte Gulf, Philippine Islands.

0800-1200 Watch: Steaming as before laying (SONO) buoys.

1648: Anchored in Leyte Gulf between Dinagat Island and Homonhon Islands, Philippine Islands. (General quarters most of the day).

11th November, Anchored as before in Leyte Gulf.

0628: Underway to install (SONO) buoys.

0955: Stopped work on (SONO) buoys to go to (general quarters).

1803: (Secured from general quarters) and anchored in Leyte Gulf between Dinagat Island and Homonhon Islands.

12th November, Anchored as before.

0623: Underway, to install (SONO) buoys.

1648: Anchored in San Pedro Bay, Leyte Gulf, Leyte, in the Philippine Islands. (General quarters most of the day).

13th November, Anchored as before. U.S.S. Fremont (LPA44) is (SOPA).

0830: Underway to go alongside the U.S.S. Indus (AKN-1).

0840: Moored alongside the U.S.S. Indus (AKN-1).

1830: Underway, proceeding to anchorage.

1855: Anchored in San Pedro Bay, Leyte Gulf, Leyte, in the Philippine Islands. (General quarters most of the day).

14th November, Anchored as before. U.S.S. Fremont (LPA44) is (SOPA).

0758: Underway, proceeding to U.S.S. Mink (IX-123) to take on fuel

0845: Moored alongside the U.S.S. Mink (IX-123)

1237: Fueling completed, underway for anchorage.

1320: Anchored in San Pedro Bay, Leyte Gulf, in the Philippine Islands.

1727: Commenced diving operations to inspect ships bottom.

1745: Diving operations completed. (General quarters most of the day).

15th November, Anchored as before. U.S.S. Fremont (LPA44) is (SOPA).

1250: U.S.S. Teak (AN35) came alongside. (General quarters most of the day).

16th November, Anchored as before with U.S.S. Teak (AN35) alongside U.S.S. Fremond (LPA44) is (SOPA).

0910: Paymaster from the U.S.S. Indus (AKN-1) came aboard to pay crew.
Note: (No entry when paymaster left ship)
(General quarters most of the day).

17th November, Anchored as before. U.S.S. Mount McKinley (AGC-7) is (SOPA).
1104: U.S.S. Teak (AN35) underway from alongside.
1116: Underway, proceeding to U.S.S. Severn (AO61)
1203: Moored alongside the U.S.S. Severn (AO61)
1250: Underway from alongside the U.S.S. Severn (AO61) and proceeding to Dulag in Leyte Gulf.
1535: Anchored off Dulag, in Leyte Gulf, Philippine Islands.
(General quarters most of the day).

18th November, Anchored as before. U.S.S. McKinlet (AGC-7) is (SOPA).
0717: Underway, to salvage a (LCM).
0730: Commenced diving operations to recover (LCM).
1207: Diving operations completed. (LCM) secured to forward horns. Underway proceeding to U.S.S. Indus (AKN-1).
1643: Moored alongside the U.S.S. Indus (AKN-1). (General quarters most of the day).

19th November, Moored as before alongside the U.S.S. Indus (AKN-1). U.S.S. Mount McKinley (AGC-7) is (SOPA).
0740: Underway to salvage operations. (No entry in log of what kind of salvage operations).
0905: Commenced salvage operations.
1507: Secured from salvage operations and underway for anchorage.
1700: Anchored in San Pedro Bay, Leyte. Philippine Islands. (General quarters off and on most of the day).

20th November, Anchored as before. U.S.S. Mount McKinlet (AGC-7) is (SOPA).
1110: Underway. (Destination not entered in log).
1525: Anchored. (Anchorage not entered in log).

1630: Underway, proceeding to go alongside the U.S.S. Triangulum (AK-102).

1810: Underway from alongside the U.S.S. Triangulum (AK-102). (No entry in log why we were alongside the Triangulum).

1815: Anchored in San Pedro Bay, between Leyte and Samar Islands. (General quarters off and on most of the day).

21st November, Anchored as before. U.S.S. Mount McKinley (AGC-7) is (SOPA).

0702: Underway to lay moorings for (ARD-19).

1900: Secured work for the day, Anchored in San Pedro Bay, Leyte Gulf, Leyte, Philippine Islands. (General quarters off and on all day).

22nd November, Anchored as before. U.S.S. Mount McKinley (AGC-7) is (SOPA).

0700: Underway to complete laying moorings for (ARD-19)

1630: Completed laying moorings for (ARD-19). Anchored in San Pedro Bay, Leyte Gulf, Leyte, in the Philippine Islands. (General quarters most of the day)

23rd to 24th November, Anchored as before. U.S.S. Mount McKinley (AGC-7) is (SOPA).

On the 24th at 0720: Underway to conduct salvage work off Samar Beach.

1230: Left the area of Samar beach and underway to assist in docking U.S.S. Ross (DD563). U.S.S. Ross hull damaged by hitting (2) mines, plus her super structure damaged by Japanese aircraft. (The history of the U.S.S. Ross (DD563) is great reading).

1422: Completed docking operation of the U.S.S. Ross (DD563). Underway and proceeding to the U.S.S. Indus (AKN-1) with LCM secured to forward horns.

1735: Anchored in San Pedro Bay, Leyte Gulf, Leyte, in the Philippine Islands. With LCM secured to forward horns. (LCM is a landing craft mechanized) (General quarters off and on all day).

25th November, Anchored as before. U.S.S. Mount McKinley

(AGD-7) is (SOPA).

0753: Underway, proceeding to the U.S.S. Indus (AKN-1) with (LCM) secured to forward horns.

0820: Moored alongside the U.S.S. Indus and off loaded (LCM).

1230: Underway to recover moorings in inter harbor.

1658: Secured from recovery operations and anchored in San Pedro Bay, Leyte Gulf, Leyte, Philippine Islands.

26ᵗʰ November, Anchored as before. U.S.S. Mount McKinley (AGC-7) is (SOPA).

0707: Underway to pick up moorings.

0715: Anchored and commenced operations of picking up moorings.

1405: Completed picking up the last of 6 moorings. Underway to pull (YDG-22) (A district degaussing vessel) off the mud flats Northwest of Bagacay Island.

1430: Anchored off mud flats

1515: (YDG-22) pulled off mud flats.

1556: Underway, for anchorage in San Pedro Bay.

1750: Anchored in San Pedro Bay, Leyte Gulf, Leyte, in the Philippine Islands. (General quarters off and on all day).

27ᵗʰ November, Anchored as before. U.S.S. Mount McKinley (AGC-7) is (SOPA).

0755: Underway to recover a stern anchor for an (LST). (No hull number in log for LST). (LST is a landing ship tank)

0930: Unable to assist (LST) in recovery of stern anchor. (No reason given in log why ship was unable to assist (LST).

1010: Underway to pull barges off beach

1325: Barge number 1 pulled off beach and brought alongside.

1625: Barge number 2 pulled off beach and brought alongside.

1703: Underway with barges 1 and 2 alongside, proceeding to U.S.S. Indus (AKN-1).

1820: Anchored in San Pedro Bay, Leyte Gulf, Leyte, in the Philippine Islands. (General quarters off and on all day).

28ᵗʰ November Anchored as before. U.S.S. Mount McKinley (AGC-7) is (SOPA).

0942: Underway, for the U.S.S. Indus (AKN-1) with barges 1 and 2 alongside.

1002: Moored alongside U.S.S. Indus (AKN-1) and transferred barges 1 and 2 to the Indus.

1303: Underway from alongside the U.S.S. Indus (AKN-1).

1608: Proceeding to U.S.S. Severn (AO61) to receive fresh water.

1618: Moored alongside the U.S.S. Severn (AO61).

1659: Underway from alongside the U.S.S. Severn (AO61). Taking on fresh water completed.

1715: Anchored in San Pedro Bay, Leyte Gulf, Leyte, in the Philippine Islands. (General quarters most of the day).

29th November, Anchored as before. U.S.S. Mount McKinley (AGC-7) is (SOPA).

1115: (LSM 20) moored alongside for repairs.

1500: (LSM 20) Underway from alongside, repairs completed.

1613: underway, proceeding to the U.S.S. Indus (AKN-1).

1650: Moored alongside the U.S.S. Indus (AKN-1) (General quarters off and on all day).

30th November, Moored as before. U.S.S. Mount McKinley (AGC-7) is (SOPA).

0113: Underway to Homonhon Island to deliver supplies to the U.S.S. Teak (AN35) and the U.S.S. Satinleaf (AN43).

0835: Moored alongside the U.S.S. Satinleaf (AN43). Tansferred all (SONO) gear to the U.S.S. Satinleaf (AN-43).

1025: Underway from alongside the U.S.S. Satinleaf (AN43). Proceeding to Dulag.

1500: Ordered to proceed to inter harbor to pick up SONO gear from the U.S.S. Drayton (DD366).

1748: Moored alongside the U.S.S. Drayton (DD366).

1755: Underway from alongside the U.S.S. Drayton (DD366).

1830: Anchored in San Pedro Bay, Leyte Gulf, Leyte, in the Philippine islands.

1st December, Anchored as before. U.S.S. Wasatch (AGC-9) is (SOPA).

0810: LSM34 moored alongside for repairs.

1430: LSM34 underway from alongside, repairs completed.

1545: Underway for regular berth in San Pedro Bay.

1559: Anchored in regular berth in San Pedro Bay, Leyte Gulf, Leyte, in the Philippine Islands.

2nd December, Anchored as before. U.S.S. Wasatch (AGC-9) is (SOPA).

0930: Underway to raise sunken (LCVP).

0955: Anchored in position to raise sunken (LCVP).

1035: Two qualified divers commenced diving operations on sunken (LCVP).

1205: Completed diving operations on sunken (LCVP).

1310: (LCVP) brought to the surface.

1515: Underway to shift berth in San Pedro Bay. (No entry in log of what happened to (LCVP) after being brought to the surface).

1732: Anchored in San Pedro Bay, Leyte Gulf, Leyte, in the Philippine Islands. (General quarters off and on all day).

3rd December, Anchored as before. U.S.S. Wasatch (AGC-9) is (SOPA).

0700: Underway, proceeding to the vicinity of the U.S.S. Stag (AW-1).

0810: Anchored in vicinity of U.S.S. Stag (AW-1).

0844: Underway to go alongside the U.S.S. Stag (AW-1) for fresh water.

0943: Moored alongside the U.S.S. Stag (AW-1).

1004: (SC 737) moored alongside.

1050: (SC 737) underway from alongside.

1051: Underway from alongside the U.S.S. Stag (AW-1)

1130: Anchored in San Pedro Bay, Leyte Gulf, Leyte, in the Philippine Islands. (General quarters off and on all day).

6th to the 7th of December, Anchored as before. U.S.S. Wasatch (AGC-9) is (SOPA).

0845: (SC 745), Alongside for repairs.

1558: (SC 745), Underway from alongside, repairs completed.

8th to the 9th of December, Anchored as before. U.S.S. Wasach (AGC-9) is (SOPA).

1305: Underway, proceeding to the U.S.S. Liddle (DE 206/APD-60) to assist in cutting away damage done to bridge and mast. (APD-60) her ridge and mast hit by Kamikaze aircraft the ship was seriously damaged. Temporary repairs made so ship can return to San Francisco to be put in dry dock for major repairs).

1400: Moored alongside U.S.S. Liddle (APD-60). In San Pedro Bay, Leyte Gulf, Leyte, in the Philippine Islands.
1645: Hoisted aboard Captain Hylants (LCVP) for repairs.

10th December to 12th December, Moored as before, alongside the U.S.S. Liddle (APD-60) in San Pedrp Bay, Leyte Gulf, Philippine Islands. U.S.S. Wasatch (AGC-9) U.S.S. Mount McKinley (AGC-7) is (SOPA).
1730: Underway from alongside the U.S.S. Liddle (APD-60). Temporary work completed.
1735: Moored in San Pedro Bay, in (berth 18), Leyte Gulf, Leyte, in the Philippine Islands.

13th December to 31st December 1944 moored as before in (berth 18). U.S.S Mount McKinley (AGC-7) is (SOPA).
(While moored in (berth 18) the following ships came alongside for repairs, (LSM23, LSM316, LSM18, LSM42, LSM38, LSM258, LSM34, LSM39, LSM51 and LSM22).

Note: This Christmas and also New Years the ship was at anchor in San Pedro Bay, Leyte Gulf, Leyte, in the Philippine Islands.

1st January 1945 Anchored as before in (berth 18), repairs completed on LSM 42.
1000: Got underway for new anchorage.
1112: Moored to (buoy 46), in San Pedro Bay, Leyte Gulf, Leyte, in the Philippine Islands.
1240: Underway to recover (750) pound anchor.

1315: Anchored to recover anchor.

1330: Commenced diving operation to recover anchor.

1410: Completed diving operations, anchor recovered.

1420: Underway to San Pedro Bay, Leyte Gulf, Leyte, in the Philippine Islands to (buoy 46).

1447: Moored to (buoy 46) in San Pedro Bay, Leyte Gulf, in the Philippine Islands.

1512: LSM316 moored alongside for repairs.

1521: LSM19 moored alongside for repairs. (General quarters off and on all day).

2nd January, Moored as before to (buoy 46). (SOPA) is Com Task Force (75) on the beach at Talosa. The (LSM 316), (LSM 19) moored alongside.

0712: (LSM 316) underway from alongside, repairs completed.

1620: (LSM 19) underway from alongside, repairs completed. (General quarters off and on all day).

3rd January, Moored as before to (buoy 46). (SOPA) is Com Task Force (75) on the beach at Talosa.

1039: (LSM 40) moored alongside for minor repairs.

1330: (LCI 983) moored alongside for minor repairs. (General quarters off and on all day).

4th January, Moored as before to (buoy 46). (SOPA) is Com Task Force (75) on the beach at Talosa. (LST 619) alongside to have screw changed. Commenced diving operations on (LST 619). (LCI 983) moored alongside for continuation of repairs.

0810: Diving operations completed of installation of new screw on (LST 619).

0820: (LST 619) underway from alongside.

0948: United States Army (RP116) (Army tug) alongside to have screw changed.

1620: Commenced diving operations to recover steel plate thrown overboard by mistake.

1745: Completed diving operations for recovery of steel plate. Steel plate not recovered. (General quarters off and on all day).

5th January, Moored as before to (buoy 46). (SOPA) is Com Task Force (75) is on the beach at Talosa. Alongside for repairs are the (LCI 983) and the United States Army (TP116).

0920: Commenced diving operations to change screw on Army (TP 116).

1230: (LCI 29) moored alongside for repairs.

1645: Secured diving operations on United States Army (TP 116). (General quarters off and on all day).

6th January, Moored as before to (buoy 46). (SOPA) is Com Task Force (75) on beach at Talosa. Alongside for repairs, (LCI 983), (LCI 29), and United States Army (TP 116).

0155: (LCI 98) underway from alongside, repairs completed. (General quarters off and on all day).

7th January, Moored as before to (buoy 46). (SOPA) is Com Task Force (75) on the beach at Talosa. (LCI 29) is alongside for repairs.

0905: Underway, proceeding to (AFD 24) (mobile floating dry dock). Left (LCI 29) moored to (buoy 42).

0930: Anchored near (AFD 24).

1125: Underway with barge alongside, proceeding to berth where (AFD 24) moorings are to be placed.

1255: Anchored with stern anchor midway between buoy (44) and buoy (45). Commenced laying 24 (AFG) moorings. (General quarters off and on all day).

8th January, Anchored as before. (SOPA) is Com Task Force (75) on the beach at Talosa.

1010: Underway to lay moorings for (AFD 24).

1700: Anchored in San Pedro Bay, Leyte.Gulf, Leyte, in the Philippine Islands. (General quarters off and on all day).

9th January, Anchored as before. (SOPA) is Com Task Force (75) on the beach at Talosa.

1024: Underway, proceeding to vicinity of the U.S.S. Oglala (ARG-1).

1320: Anchored near (ARD 19).

1435: underway, proceeding to Tacloban harbor with two barges in tow. (No entry in log to where barges came from)
1729: Anchored in San Juanixo Strain, off Amibong point.
1748: Anchored two barges.
1755: Underway, proceeding out of Tacloban harbor.
1855: Anchored in San Pedro Bay in (berth 218). Leyte Gulf, Leyte, in the Philippine Islands.

11th January, Anchored as before. (SOPA) is Com Task Force (75) on the beach at Talosa.
0710: Underway to lay moorings for (ARD-7).
1100: At work laying moorings.
1900: Ceased laying moorings for (ARD-7) and underway for anchorage.
1949: Anchored in San Pedro Bay, Leyte Gulf, Philippine Islands.

12th January, Anchored as before. (SOPA) is Con Task Force (75) on the beach at Talosa.
0740: Underway to lay moorings for (ARD-7).
0945: Commenced laying moorings for (ARD-7)/
1509: Anchored off (ARD-7) in San Pedro Bay, Leyte Gulf, Leyte, in the Philippine Islands.

13th January, Anchored as before. (SOPA) is Com Task Force (75) on the beach at Talosa.
0744: Underway, proceeding to (ARD-7) to complete moorings.
0810: Commenced work on laying moorings for (ARD-7).
0945: Completed mooring (ARD-7). Underway, proceeding to the U.S.S. Caribou (IX114)(tanker)
0950: Alongside the U.S.S. Caribou (IX114) to do small welding job.
1112: Completed welding job, underway proceeding to anchorage.
1127: Moored to (buoy 46) in San Pedro Bay, LeyteGulf, Leyte, in the Philippine Islands.

14th January, Moored as before. (SOPA) Con Task Force (75) on the beach at Talosa.
1230: Underway, and proceeding to the U.S.S. Shikellamy (AO-90)

to take on fuel.

1430: Fueling completed, underway from alongside the U.S.S. Shikellamy (AO-90) and proceeding to the U.S.S. Carondelet (IX136) to assist in moving a 4 ton evaporator.

1500: Moored alongside the U.S.S. Carondelet (IX136) to assist in moving evaporator.

1620: Completed assigned job at the U.S.S. Carondelet (IX136).

1630: Underway, proceeding to the U.S.S. Stag (AW-1) for fresh water.

1730: Completed taking on fresh water, underway from alongside the U.S.S. Stag (AW-1) proceeding to (buoy 46).

1835: Moored to buoy in berth 46 in San Pedro Bay, Leyte Gulf, Leyte, in the Phillipine Islands.

15th to the 16th January, Moored as before to (buoy 46) in San Pedro Bay. (SOPA) is Com Task Force (75) on the beach at Talosa.

0745: Underway, proceeding to (AFD-11).

0810: Anchored, commenced to lay moorings for (AFD-11).

1405: Underway, for a new location.

1520: Anchored, operating as before.

1806: Underway, proceeding to anchorage.

1820: Anchored in San Pedro Bay, Leyte Gulf, Leyte, in the Philippine Islands.

17th January, Anchored as before.

1015: Underway, proceeding to (AFD-11), to assist in laying moorings.

1605: Completed mooring (AFD-11), underway, proceeding to buoy in berth 46.

1755: Moored to (buoy 46) in San Pedro Bay, Leyte Gulf, Leyte, in the Philippine Islands.

18th and 20th January, Shifted berths, from (buoy 46) to (buoy 62), with (LCT 992) alongside for repairs. (No entry in log when (LCT 992) came alongside for repairs?).

0800: (LCT 992) underway from alongside, repairs completed. (LSM 35) came alongside for minor repairs.

1031: (LSM 35) cast off, her minor repairs completed. (LSM 205) and (LSM 217) came alongside for minor repairs.
1725: Completed diving operations on (LSM 205). Operation on (LSM 205) was for changing her screw.

21st January, Moored as before to (buoy 62) in San Pedro Bay, Leyte Gulf, Leyte, in the Philippine Islands.
(LSM 217) came alongside for repairs.
1745: (LSM 169) is alongside for repairs
1245: (LSM 169) underway from alongside, her repairs are completed.
1515: (LSM 317) is alongside for minor repairs.
1620: (LSM 315) alongside (LSM 317) for minor repairs
1800: (LSM 315) is underway from alongside.

22nd January, Moored as before to (buoy 62) in San Pedro Bay, Leyte Gulf, Leyte, in the Philippine Islands. Alongside for repairs are (LSM 217) and (LSM 317).
0740: (LSM 317) Underway from alongside her repairs completed.
0805: (LSM 315) back alongside to finish minor repairs.
1235: (LSM 315) underway from alongside.
1245: (LSM 315) moored outboard of barge. (No description of barge or location of barge).
1305: (LSM 217) alongside for repairs.
1315: Commenced diving operations on (LSM 217) to change screw.
1432: Ceased diving operations.
1829: (LSM 31) underway from barge.

23rd January, Moored as before to (buoy 62) in San Pedro Bay, Leyte Gulf, Leyte, in the Philippine Islands. (LSM 217) is alongside for repairs.
0445: Commenced diving operations on (LSM 217) to finish changing screw.
1013: Diving operations completed (LSM 217).
1040: (LSM 217) underway from alongside, all repairs completed.
1100: (LSM 258) alongside for repairs.
1224: Salvage barge (No 1) with (LCC-C1) in skids came alongside.

(No entry in log to explain where barge of (LCC-C1) came from or what happened to them).
1235: (LSM 5) alongside for repairs.
1403: (LSM 258) underway from alongside.
1421: Repairs on (LSM 317) almost completed.

24th January, Moored as before to (buoy 62) in San Pedro Bay, Leyte Gulf, Leyte, in the Philippine Islands.
(LSM 54) and (LSM 317) came alongside for repairs.
0804: (LSM 54) repairs completed, underway from alongside.
1001: (LSM 317) repairs completed, underway from alongside.
1120: (LSM 219) alongside for repairs.
1230: (LSM 237) moored outboard of (LSM 219) for repairs.
1325: LSM (217) alongside for repairs.
1615: Commenced diving operations on (LSM 217) to change screw.
2310: Completed diving operations on (LSM 217).

25th January, Moored as before to (buoy 62) in San Pedro Bay, Leyte Gulf, Leyte, in the Philippine Islands. (LSM 217), (LSM 219) and (LSM 237) are alongside for repairs.
0657: (LSM 217) underway from alongside, repairs completed.
0748: (LSM 237) underway from alongside, repairs completed.
0830: (LSM 269) alongside for minor repairs.
1310: (LSM 219) moved from portside to starboard side for minor repairs.
1430: (LSM 39) alongside for repairs.

26th January, Moored as before to (buoy 62) in San Pedro Bay, Leyte Gulf, Leyte, in the Philippine Islands. With (LSM 269), (LSM 39) and (LSM 219) are alongside for repairs.
0709: Completed repairs on (LSM 39), (LSM 39) underway from alongside (LSM 269).
0822: (LSM 219) shifted to outboard of (LSM 269).
1245: Commenced diving operations on (LSM 269) using divers from the U.S.S. Otus (AG-20). Divers commenced changing screw on (LSM 269).
1415: Completed diving operations on (LSM 269).

1755: (SC 729) alongside for minor repairs. (SC stands for Sub chaser).

27th January, Moored as before to (buoy 62) in San Pedro Bay, Leyte Gulf, Leyte, in the Philippine Islands. With (LSM 269), (LSM 219) and (SC 729) are alongside for repairs.
0415: (SC 729) underway from alongside, repairs completed.
0810: (LSM 420) alongside for minor repairs.
1724: (LSM 42) underway from alongside, repairs completed.

28th January, Moored as before to (buoy 62) in San Pedro Bay, Leyte Gulf, Leyte, in the Philippine Islands. With (LSM 219) and (LSM 269) are alongside for repairs.
1515: (LSM 22) alongside for minor repairs.
1630: Commenced diving operations on (LSM 22) to change screw.
1720: Completed diving operations on (LSM 22).
1723: (LSM 22) underway from alongside, repairs completed.

29th January, Moored as before to (buoy 62) in San Pedro Bay, Leyte Gulf, in the Philippine Islands. With (LSM 219) and (LSM 269) are alongside for repairs.
0700: (LSM 219) and (LSM 269) underway from alongside, repairs completed.

0710: Underway, proceeding to (ARD-7) to put ship in dry dock for hull inspection and to scrap hull and paint hull from main deck to keel.

0942: Entered (ARD-7).
1025: Ship resting on keel blocks.

U.S.S. Silverbell (AN-51) in (ARD-7). With seaman Troy Cole looking over the side at shipmates scraping the hull.

30th January to the 31st: Ship resting on keel blocks in (ARD-7) in San Pedro Bay, Leyte Gulf, Leyte, in the Philippine Islands.

While ship was resting on keel blocks in dry dock at (0730) on this day. A great History Making event was taking place in central Luzon, Philippine Islands. Members of the Army's elite Sixth Ranger Battalion, (120) rangers and Army Alamo scouts and with Filipino Guerrillas. At (0730) this rescue group was attacking the Cabanatuan prison to rescue (512) prisoners of war. The fight lasted (30) minutes. All (512) prisoners made it out the gate some with the help of their rescuers.

Also this is the place our divers in the first part of the story were taken after all diving was stop, and where they spend the rest of the war under condition that would make you sick.

A great reference for this rescue is a book titled "The Great Raid".

0815: Commenced flooding dry dock
0900: Underway from (ARD-7), hull inspection and painting completed.
0910: Anchored in San Pedro Bay, Leyte Gulf, Leyte, in the Philippine Islands.

1116: Underway for Guian Harbor, Samar, in the Philippine Islands.
1159: Picked up (8) men from the U.S.S. Satinleaf (AN 43) for
transportation to Guian.
1720: Anchored in Guian harbor, Samar, in the Philippine Islands.
1800: Transferred (8) men to the receiving station at Guian.

1st February to 2nd February, Ship anchored as before in Guian
Harbor, Samar, in the Philippine Islands.
0826: Underway, proceeding to inner harbor.
1255: Moored to (buoy 62) in San Pedro Bay, Leyte Gulf, in the
Philippine Islands.

3rd February, Moored as before to (buoy 62) in San Pedro Bay.
1030: Underway, proceeding to Tarraguna with barge in tow to
salvage (LCT) ramp.
1305: Arrived Tarraguna.
1835: Anchored off Tarraguna in Leyte Gulf, Leyte, in the Philippine
Islands.

4th February, Anchored as before off Tarraguna, in Leyte Gulf, Leyte,
in the Philippine Islands.
1055: Underway to raise (LCT) ramp.
1158: Anchored to start salvage operations.
1300: Ramp brought to surface. (No entry in log as how ramp was
recovered from bottom of harbor).
1350: Ramp placed on deck of (LCT 679).
1432: Underway, proceeding to anchorage in San Pedro Bay,
1732: Anchored in San Pedro Bay, Leyte Gulf, Leyte, in the
Philippine Islands.
2100: Hoisted (LCVP No. 2) aboard because it was in sinking
condition.

5th February, Anchored as before in San Pedro Bay. (No entry in log
has what happened to (LCVP No 2).
1350: Underway, for salvage operations.
1648: Anchored off Yellow Beach in Leyte Gulf, Leyte, in the
Philippine Islands.

6th February, Anchored as before off Yellow Beach in Leyte Gulf, Leyte, in the Philippine Islands.

0830: Commenced diving operations. (No entry in log of what kind of diving operation).

1200: Secured from diving operations.

1300: Commenced diving operations. (No description of what kind of diving operations.

1500: Secured from diving operations.

1550: Underway to pick up (LVT-A-4).

1815: Underway, proceeding to Dulog with tank and barge in tow. (No entry in log to what happened to tank and barge of where it was picked up at).

1930: Anchored off Yellow Beach 2 miles south of Dulog in Leyte Gulf, Leyte, in the Philippine Islands.

2035: Cast off LVT-A-4) for transportation to the beach. (No entry in log of where LVT-A-4) was picked up at).

2050: (LVT-A-4) took on water and sank.

7th February, Anchored as before off Yellow Beach 2 miles South of Dulog in Leyte Gulf, Leyte, in the Philippine Islands.

0913: Underway to continue salvage operations on (LVT-A-4).

0922: Anchored, commenced diving operations to salvage (LVT-A-4).

1015: Completed diving operations. (No entry in log to what happened to (LVT-A-4).

1126: Underway, proceeding to anchorage in San Pedro Bay, Letye Gulf, Leyte, in the Philippine Islands.

1415: Anchored in San Pedro Bay, Leyte Gulf, Leyte, in the Philippine Islands.

8th, 9th and 10th February, Anchored as before in San Pedro Bay, Leyte Gulf, Leyte, in the Philippine Islands.

1742: Underway, proceeding to the U.S.S. Wildcat (AW-2) to take on water.

1808: Alongside the U.S.S. Wildcat (AW-2).

1850: Completed taking on water.

1853: Underway, from alongside the U.S.S. Wildcat (AW-2).

Proceeding to anchorage in San Pedro Bay.
1940: Anchored in San Pedro Bay, Leyte Gulf, Leyte, in the
Philippine Islands.

11th February to 21st February, Anchored in Guian Roadstead, Samar,
Philippine Islands and San Pedro Bay, Leyte Gulf, Leyte, Philippine
Islands. Changed anchorage (2) times, no reason given for changes of
anchorage. U.S.S. Butternut (AN-9) came alongside on the (15th of
February). No entry why she was alongside and no entry for when she
got underway from alongside.

17th of February
1324: The U.S.S. Silverbell (AN-51) got underway to lay markers for
net line. No entry for completion of laying markers for net line

19th February commenced laying moorings for (YFD-64).

21st February completed laying moorings for (YFD-64).
1404: Underway for Lauaan Bay, Leyte Gulf, In the Philippine
Islands.
1700: Anchored in Lavaan Bay, Leyte Gulf, in the Philippine Islands.

22nd February, Anchored as before in Lavaan Bay, Leyte Gulf, Leyte,
in the Philippine Islands.
0802: (YW-90) underway from alongside after discharging fresh
water. (No entry in log to when (YW-90) came alongside).
1037: Underway, proceeding to Guian Roadstead, Samar, in the
Philippine Islands.
1535: Anchored in Guian Roadstead, Samar, in the Philippine
Islands.

23rd February, Anchored as before.
1640: (5) men reported aboard from the U.S.S. Torchwood (AN-55)
for temporary duty.

24th February, Anchored as before U.S.S. San Clemente (AG-79) is
(SOPA).

0840: Got underway with net barge in tow. (No log entry where net barge came from or when it came alongside)
1125: Anchored in Guian Roadstead, Samar, in the Philippine Islands. (No entry in log to what happen to net barge).

25th February, Anchored as before.
0840: Underway, proceeding to Guian Roadstead, Samar, in the Philippine Islands.
0852: Anchored by stern anchor and bow moored to net barge in Guian Roadstead, Samar. Philippine Islands.

26th to the 27th of February, Anchored as before by stern anchor and bow moored to net barge in Guian Roadstead, Samar, Philippine Islands.

27th February
1615: Commenced diving operation. (No description in log of what kind of diving operations).
1840: Secured from diving operations. (No entry in log if diving operations were completed)

28th February, Anchored as before with stern anchor and bow moored to net barge in Guian Roadstead, Samar, in the Philippine Islands.
0820: Lt Comdr. Dittmann, (CTU 72.4.1)(Commander Task Unit) left ship to go aboard the U.S.S. Butternut (AN-9). (No entry in ship's log, when Comdr. Dittmann came aboard or why he was aboard).

1105: Hoisted blue (LCVP) aboard, resting on deck on the forecastle.
1123: Underway, proceeding to San Pedro Bay, Leyte Gulf, Leyte, in the Philippine Islands.
1502: Anchored in San Pedro Bay, Leyte Gulf, Leyte, in the Philippine Islands.
1516: Took (LCVP) from forecastle and put (LCVP) in water. (No entry in log to what happened to (LCVP) or why she was aboard and why take to San Pedro Bay).
1525: Underway, proceeding to Tacloban, San Pedro Bay. (Tacloban is the Capital of Leyte).

San Juanico Straits, in the Philippine Islands

1710: Anchored in San Juanico Straits, Philippine Islands. The San Juanico Straits is the world's narrowest straits. The Straits lies between the Islands of Samar and the Island of Leyte.

At this location the ships crew started the offloading of small arms and ammunitions to Philippine guerilla fighter Captain Ramon Magsaysay and his men. The Captain and his men came along side in outriggers to take the small arms and ammunition ashore.

No time in the ships log when the offloading was completed. A member of the crew said it took hours to offload due to the amount of the ammunition and small arms that could be loaded in the outriggers. There was more than one outrigger in this operation. As one was completed another came along side and took its place. It was way into the night when the transfer of the cargo was completed.

Note:

Captain Ramon Magsaysay was born August 31ˢᵗ, 1907 and died on March 17ᵗʰ, 1957 in an airplane crash.

He entered the University of the Philippines in 1927. He worked as a chauffeur to support himself as he studied engineering; later, he transferred to the Institute of Commerce at Rizal College (1928-1932), where he received a baccalaureate in commerce. He then worked as an automobile mechanic and shop superintendent. When World War 11 broke out, he joined the motor pool of the 31st Infantry Division of the Philippine Army.

When Bataan surrendered in 1942, Magsaysay escaped to the hills, organized the Western Luzon Guerrilla Forces, and was commissioned Captain on 5th April 1942. For three years Captain Magsaysay operated under Col. Merrill's famed guerrilla outfit. Magsaysay was among those instrumental in clearing the Zambales coast of the Japanese prior to the landing of American forces together with the Philippine Commonwealth troops on 29th January 1945.

23rd April 1946 Magsaysay was elected as an Independent to the Philippine House of Representatives. He served two terms in the house.

Magsaysay was appointed Secretary of Defence on the 31st August 1950. Then on 10th November, 1953 Magsaysay was decisively elected the 7th president of the Philippines. He was the first to be sworn into office wearing the Barong Tagalog shirt. He then was called "Mambo Magsaysay". Under his leadership the Philippines ranked number two in Asia's clean and well-governed countries.

A Barong Tagalog shirt made famous by president Magsaysay.

28th February
1720: Put the motor launch in the water after the offloading of the cargo was completed. The boat was then brought along the starboard side and tied up.

1st March, Anchored as before in San Juanico Straits, Philippine Islands.

0725: Hoisted motor launch aboard and made preparations for getting underway.

0735: Underway, proceeding to U.S.S. Shickellamy (AOG-47) to take on fuel.

0820: Moored alongside to U.S.S. Shickellamy (AOG-47) commenced taking on fuel.

1027: Fueling completed, underway from alongside the U.S.S. Shickellamy (AOG-47) and proceeding to the U.S.S. Wildcat (AW-2) to take on fresh water.

1059: Moored alongside the U.S.S. Wildcat (AW-2) commenced taking on fresh water.

1135: Taking on fresh water completed, underway from alongside the U.S.S. Wildcat (AW-2).

1150: Anchored astern to the U.S.S. Wildcat (AW-2).

1237 to 1500: Underway and alongside the U.S.S. Wildcat (AW-2) to take on board a LCVP. Secured LCVP down and proceeded to inner harbor.

1620: Anchored in San Juanico Straits, Philippine Islands.

1820: U.S.S. Teaberry (AN-34) came alongside.

2nd March, Anchored as before in San Juanico Straits, Philippine Islands with the U.S.S. Teaberry (AN-34) alongside.

1425: Underway, proceeding to San Pedro Bay, Leyte Gulf, Leyte, in the Philippine Islands. (No entry in log, when U.S.S. Teaberry (AN-34) got underway).

1550: Anchored in San Pedro Bay, Leyte Gulf, Leyte, in the Philippine Islands.

2240: U.S.S. Teaberry (AN-34) came alongside.

3rd March, Anchored as before in San Pedro Bay, Leyte Gulf, Leyte, in the Philippine Islands. With U.S.S. Teaberry (AN-34) alongside.

0827: U.S.S. Teaberry (AN-34) underway from alongside.

0831: Underway, proceeding to anchor convoy at Tolosa, Leyte Gulf, Leyte, in the Philippine Islands.

0953: Convoy anchored at, Tolosa, Leyte Gulf, Leyte, in the

Philippine Islands.

4th March, Anchored as before, in convoy anchorage, Tolosa, Leyte Gulf, Leyte, in the Philippine Islands.
1137: Underway, proceeding to take proper position in convoy. (No convoy number in log).
1240, Took proper position in convoy. Proceeding by San Pedro Bay, Leyte Gulf, Leyte, to Subic Bay, Luzon, in the Philippine Islands.

4th March to 7th March Steaming in convoy as before.

7th March
1716: The convoy disbanded. All convoy ships steaming independently to entry into Subic Bay, Luzon. Philippine Islands.

Grande Island at entrance to Subic Bay, Luzon, Philippine Islands. One passes to the left of Island when entering the bay.

The construction of Subic Bay, Luzon, in the Philippine Islands, after World War 11, Grande Island in upper left of picture.

1830: Moored alongside the U.S.S. Indus (AKN-1) in berth ((192).
1900: U.S.S. Teaberry (AN-34) moored alongside.

8th March, Moored as before alongside the U.S.S. Indus (AKN-1) with the U.S.S. Teaberry (AN-34) along our starboard side. (SOPA) is the U.S.S. Blue Ridge (AGC-2).
0712: Underway from alongside the U.S.S. Indus (AKN-1). (No entry in log, to what time U.S.S. Teaberry (AN-34) got underway from alongside).
0723: Anchored astern of the U.S.S. Indus (AKN-1).
1225: Underway, proceeding to new anchorage.
1245: Anchored in Subic Bay, Luzon. Philippine Islands.
1430: (LSM 54) came alongside for underwater repairs.
1500: Commenced diving operations on (LSM 54) to change screw.
2200: Secured diving operations on (LSM 54).

9th March, Anchored as before in Subic Bay, Luzon, Philippine Islands. With the (LSM 54) alongside for underwater repairs.
0812: Commenced diving operations on (LSM 54), to change screw.
1600: Diving operations completed on (LSM 54).
1605: (LSM 54) underway from alongside.

1635: (LSM 66) came alongside for underwater repairs. (Screw change) Commenced diving operations on (LSM 66).
2200: Secured diving operations on (LSM 66).

10th March, Anchored as before. (LSM 66) is alongside for underwater repairs.
0815: Commenced diving operations on (LSM 66) to change screw.
1908: Completed diving operation (LSM 66).

11th March, Anchored as before in Subic Bay, Luzon. Philippine Islands. (LSM 66) moored alongside. (SOPA) is the Blue Ridge (AGC-2).
0850: (LSM 66) underway from alongside.

11th March to 27th March, Began the installation of (A/T) nets at entrance to Subic Bay, Luzon. Philippine Islands.

24th March,
0730: Underway to go alongside the U.S.S. Gilmore (AS-11) (sub tender) to have evaporators cleaned.
0828: Moored along side the U.S.S. Ligarbo. Which is alongside the U.S.S. Gilmore (AS-11). U.S.S. Blue Ridge (AGC-2) is (SOPA).
1617: Cleaning completed, underway to anchorage
1705: Anchored in Subic Bay, Luzon, in the Philippine Islands.

28th March, Anchored in Subic Bay, Luzon. Philippine Islands. U.S.S. Blue Ridge (AGC-2) is (SOPA).
0808: Underway, proceeding to the U.S.S. Stag (AW-1) to take on fresh water.
0850: Moored alongside the U.S.S. Stag (AW-1).
0940: Completed taking on water, underway from alongside and proceeding to net line.
1145: Underway from net line and proceeding to anchorage.
1207: Anchored in regular berth in Subic Bay, Luzon. Philippine Islands.

29th March, Anchored as before in Subic Bay, Luzon. U.S.S. Blue Ridge (AGC-2) is (SOPA).

0700: Underway, proceeding to Manila Bay, Luzon. Philippine Islands.

1130: Anchored in Mariveles Harbor, Luzon. Philippine Islands.

1400: Underway, proceeding to Corregidor

1500: Anchored off Corregidor. (No entry in log why we anchored off Corregidor).

1805: Underway, proceeding to Mariveles Harbor, Luzon. Philippine Islands.

1855: Anchored in Mariveles harbor, Luzon. Philippine Islands.

30th March, Anchored as before.

0650: Underway, proceeding to Manila Bay, Luzon. Philippine Islands.

1121: Anchored in Manila Bay, Luzon. Philippine Islands.

31st March, Anchored as before.

0830: Underway, proceeding to Subic Bay, Luzon. Philippine Islands.

1440: Entering Subic Bay, Luzon. Philippine Islands.

1458: Anchored in Subic Bay, Luzon. Philippine Islands. U.S.S. Blue Ridge (AGC-2) is (SOPA).

1stApril to10th April,
Ship anchored as before in Subic Bay, Luzon. Philippine Islands. U.S.S. Blue Ridge (AGC-2) (SOPA is (CTF 78)

10th April

0800: Underway to coal dock in Subic Bay to take on fresh water.

0900: Moored starboard side to U.S.S. Teaberry (AN-34) to take on fresh water from dock.

0935: (LCI 957) came along Portside to take on fresh water from coal dock.

1031: (LCI 957) underway from alongside, taking on fresh water completed.

1032: Underway, per orders from (CNB) (Commander Naval Base

Subic Bay, Luzon, Philippine Islands) to proceed to Manila Bay, Luzon, Philippine Islands.

1818: Anchored in berth (127) at the south end of breakwater in Manila Bay, Luzon. Philippine Islands.

Note:

Upon entering Manila Bay it was a scene of sunken Japanese ships by the hundreds littering the large harbor. The naval ships were escort ships smaller than a destroyer, and the rest were merchantmen. Manila Bay was shallow and the superstructures of the sunken ships were above water. Many of these still had Japanese aboard, and if someone got to close, they would draw rifle fire.

11th April: Anchored as before in berth (127) at south end of breakwater in Manila Bay, Luzon. Philippine Islands.

11th April

(0000-0400) The ship engaged in receiving and servicing (LCVP's) from the SS Black Jack. (Contracted oil tanker).

0315: Completed servicing (7-LCVP's) from the SS Black Jack.

0745: *Starboard liberty party left ship for Manila, the first liberty since leaving the States* in 1944.

0947: US Army (P-443) alongside for fuel.

1010: Fueling completed, US Army (P-443) underway from alongside.

1215: Starboard liberty party returned to ship.

1245: *Port liberty party left ship for Manila.*

1640: (LST 698) alongside for fuel.

1740: Port liberty party returned to ship.

Note: The Silverbells favorite watering hole in Manila was the " Pink Elephant".

1942: Fueling completed, (LST 698) underway from alongside.
2000: Anchored as before in (berth 127) at south end of breakwater, in Manila Bay, Luzon. Philippine Islands with (8) (LCVP's) moored alongside.

12th April to 13th April, Anchored as before in berth (127). U.S.S. Romback (DE364) is (SOPA).

13 April
1025 to 1050: Shifted anchorage in Manila Bay, Luzon. Philippine Islands.

13th April
1151: Colors order at half-mast for 30 days in honor of the death of President
Franklin D. Roosevelt.

14th April to 15th of April, Anchored as before in berth (127), Manila Bay, Luzon. Philippine Islands. U.S.S. Romback (DE-364) is (SOPA).

15th of April
0645: Got underway and proceeding to Subic Bay, Luzon, in the Philippine Islands, in the company with (LCI)
1007: Also with the convoy are small craft, (LCVP'S) and (LSM'S).
0818: Took (LCVP) in tow.
0840: Took (LCM) (L-68) in tow.
1407: Passed through entrance (A/T) net gate to Subic Bay, Luzon. Philippine Islands.
1510: Anchored in Subic Bay, Luzon. Philippine Islands. U.S.S. Blue Ridge (AGC-2) is (SOPA).

16th April, Anchored as before in Subic Bay, Luzon. Philippine Islands. (U.S.S. Blue Ridge) (AGC-2) is (SOPA).
1108: Underway, proceeding to the U.S.S. Kenwood (IX-179) to take on fuel.
1205: Moored alongside the U.S.S. Kenwood (IX-179), commenced

to take on fuel.

1338: Fueling completed, underway and proceeding to anchorage.

1432: Anchored in Subic Bay, Luzon. Philippine Islands.

17th April, Anchored as before in Subic Bay, Luzon. Philippine Islands. (U.S.S. Blue Ridge) (AGC-2) is (SOPA).

17th of April

0805: Underway to Olongopo Section of Subic Bay, Luzon, in the Philippine Islands.

0830: Anchored in Olongopo section of Subic Bay.

1408: Engaged in pulling pilings, near dock, secured operations at (1953). Anchored in Olongopo section of Subic Bay.

18th April

1011: Underway back to dock area for more salvage operations of pulling more pilings and other debris near fleet post office landing and at (1636) secured from salvage operations.

19th April:

0800: Commenced salvage operations near fleet post office landing.

1700: Secured from salvage operations.

20th April

0758: Got underway to take on fresh water.

0835: moored alongside (LCT 1167) at coal dock to take on fresh water from dock.

0850: (LCT 834) came alongside.

0958: Completed taking on fresh water, go underway with (LCT 1167) alongside. (No entry in log to what happened to (LCT 834).

1005: (LCT 1167) got underway operations on sunken barge.

1245: commenced diving operations on sunken barge.

1705: Secured diving operations.

21st April

U.S.S. Dobbin (AD-3)(destroyer tender) is (SOPA).

0815 Commenced diving operations on sunken barge.

1205: completed diving operations on sunken barge. (No entry in log to what happened to sunken barge).

1220: Underway shifting anchorage to area of sunken airplane.

1300: Anchored and commenced diving operations on sunken airplane.

1657: Secured from diving operation on airplane.

22nd April, Still working on sunken airplane.

23rd April

0855: Ship underway for new anchorage. (No entry log has to what happen to sunken airplane or when diving was completed).

0920: Anchored in Subic Bay, Luzon. Philippine Islands.

23rd to 24th April, Anchored is Subic Bay, Luzon. Philippine Islands. The U.S.S. Blue Ridge (AGC-2) is (SOPA).

25th April to 29th April, Anchored as before in Subic Bay, Luzon. Philippine Islands. The U.S.S. Dobbin (AD-3) is (SOPA).

30th April: Anchored as before (SOPA) is still the U.S.S. Dobbin (AD-3).

0700: Underway, proceeding to Manila Bay, Luzon. Philippine Islands.

0741: Passed through net gate, at entrance to Subic Bay, Luzon.

1303: Entered Manila Bay, Luzon. Philippine Islands.

1540: Anchored in berth (67), in Manila Bay, Luzon, Philippine Islands.

1st May, Anchored as before in (berth 67) in Manila Bay, Luzon. Philippine Islands. The U.S.S. Currituck (AV-7) is (SOPA) (a seaplane tender).

0627: Underway, proceeding to go alongside the U.S.S. Lavaca (APA-180) to receive draft of personnel and their gear.

0640: Moored alongside the U.S.S. Lavaca (APA-180) commenced taken on (draft #386) which is (236) enlisted men and (28) officers and their gear for transportation to Subic bay, Luzon. Philippine Islands.

0952: Underway, proceeding to Subic Bay, Luzon. Philippine Islands with draft personnel aboard and gear. Set convoy formation with U.S.S. Silverbell (AN-51) as (OCT) (officer-in-tactical command). With (LCI's 1007, 578 and 637) and two (PCE)'s as escorts. (There is no entry in log that shows hull numbers for (PCE's).

1713: Entered Subic Bay, Luzon. Philippine Islands.

1741: Alongside the U.S.S. Mountpelier (C-57) to discharge draft of (236) enlisted men and (28) officers and their gear. The men then were taken to various ships in the harbor.

1900: Underway from alongside the Mountpelier (C-57). Proceeding to anchorage in Subic Bay, Luzon.

1935: Anchored in Subic Bay, Luzon. Philippine Islands.

2nd May, Anchored as before.

1300: Underway, proceeding to the U.S.S. Salamonie (AO-26) to take on fuel.

1435: Moored alongside the U.S.S. Salamonie (AO-26) commenced taking on fule.

1529: Fueling completed underway from alongside the U.S.S. Salamonie (AO-26) proceeding to anchorage.

1603: Anchored in Subic Bay, Luzon. Philippine Islands. U.S.S. Dobbin (AD-3) is (SOPA).

Note: May 2nd 1945 German troops surrendered in Italy.

3rd of May, Anchored as before.

4th May to 5th May, Anchored as before in Subic Bay, Luzon. Philippine Islands. The U.S.S. Blue Ridge (AGC-2) is (SOPA).

5th of May

0411: Convoy (NLY-121) underway with (LST 206), (FS 315), (Army cargo ship, manned by the United States Coast Guard) and (SC 981) out of Subic Bay, Luzon. Philippine Islands. Convoy (NLY-121) is in route to Seedler Harbor, Manus Island

Admiralty Islands.

1731: (LST 206) Joined convoy NLY-121 in route to Seedler Harbor, Manus Island Admiralty Islands.

1815: U.S.S. Silverbell (AN-51) joined convoy NLY-121, and is assigned to station #13. (OTC) is the (LST 635).

Note:

May 7[th]1945 unconditional surrender of all German forces to the Allies.

6th May to 8th May, Steaming in convoy (NLY-121).

Note:

8th May 1945, V.E. (Victory in Europe) Day. The U.S.S. Silverbell (AN-51) at sea.

8th May, Left convoy (NLY-121) to join convoy (IG-214).

8th of May

1545: Steaming various and speeds to join convoy (IG-214) at station (#115). (OTC) is SS Copiagsa. (Convoy IG-214) is proceeding on to Seedler Harbor, Manus Island, in the Admiralty Islands.

11th May, Steaming in convoy (IG-214).

11th May

1650, Detached from convoy (IG-214) commenced steaming singly for Seedler Harbor, Manus Island, in the Admiralty Islands.

12th May to 15th May, Steaming singly for Seedler Harbor, Manus Island. Admiralty Islands.

15th May

1320: Entered Seedler Harbor, Manus. Admiralty Islands.

1440: Anchored in (berth 254) in Seedler Harbor, Manus Island. Admiralty Islands.

16th May, Anchored as before in berth (254), in Seedler Harbor, Manus Island. Admiralty islands. To commenced three weeks of availability for overhaul.

1130: Shifting berth to repair basin inner harbor of Seedler Harbor, Manus Island, Admiralty Islands.

1228: Anchored in repair basin in inner harbor of Seedler Harbor, Manus Island, Admiralty

17th May, Anchored as before in repair basin in inner harbor of Seedler Harbor, Manus Island, Admiralty Islands.

0920: Underway, proceeding to (LST 700) in inner harbor.

0930: Moored alongside (LST 700) in inner harbor. The U.S.S. Sierra (AD-18) (destroyer tender) is (SOPA).

18th May, Moored as before, alongside (LST 700).

1453: Tug (463) made fast alongside.

19th May, Moored as before, alongside (LST 700) and Tug (463) alongside.

20th May, Moored as before, alongside (LST 700). (No entry in log to what happen to tug (463).

21st May, Moored as before, alongside (LST 700).

0958: U.S.S. Takelma (ATF-113).

1011: Cast off from (LST 700), being towed to new berth alongside dock.

1025: Moored to repair dock, at Lombrum point, Los Negros Island. Admiralty Islands. With U.S.S. Takelma (ATF-113) alongside.

22nd May, Moored as before alongside repair dock at Lombrum Point. With U.S.S. Takelma (ATF-113) alongside.

23rd May to 25th May, Moored to repair dock, at Lombrum Point, Los Negros Island. Admiralty Islands.

25th May
0854: U.S.S Takelma (ATF-113) underway from alongside.
0855: (YO-13) came alongside.
0923: (YW-101) came alongside.

26th May, Moored as before, at repair dock at Lombrum Point, Los Negros Island, Admiralty Islands, with (YO-13) and (YW-101) tied up alongside. (No entry in log to what happen to (YW-101).

28th May, Moored as before at repair dock at Lombrum Point, Los Negros Island, Admiralty Islands. With (YO-13) still moored alongside.

29th May, Moored as before, at repair dock at Lombrum Point, Los Negros Island. Admiralty Islands. With (YO-13) still moored alongside.

1001: HMS Reserve is now a (RAN) tug (loaned to the Royal Australian Navy from the British Royal Navy) she came alongside to tow us to (ABSD #4) (No entry in log to what happen to YO-13). (RAN) stands for Royal Australian Navy)

1218: (RAN) tug cast off from alongside.
1220: Entered (ABSD #4).
1404: Resting on keel blocks in (ABSD #4) with U.S.S. Hilo (AGP-2) a (PT tender), (LST 458), (LST 204) in Seedler Harbor, Manus Island. Admiralty Islands.

30th May to 3rd June, In (ABSD#4) as before.

3rd June
1237: Commenced flooding dry dock, making preparations to undock.
 1440: Cleared (ABSD #4), ship is in tow by (YT-235).
1700: Moored to U.S.S. Hilo (AGP-2) at repair dock at Lumbrum Point, Los Negros Island. Admiralty Islands.

3rd June to 6th June, Ship moored as before to repair dock at Lumbrum Point, Los Negros Island. Admiralty Islands. With U.S.S. Hilo (AGP-2) alongside.

6th June
0735: (LCM) came alongside to move ship away from U.S.S Hilo (AGP-2) so she can get underway. (LCM) moved ship out board of (LST 465) at repair dock Lumbrum Point, Los Negros Island, Admiralty Islands.

6th June to 10th of June, Moored as before out board of (LST 465) at repair dock at Lumbrum Point, Los Negros Island, Admiralty islands.

10th June
0800: Moved out from dock to let (LST 465) get underway from repair dock.
0830: Moored to repair dock at Lumbrum Point, Los Negros Island. Admiralty Islands.
1445: Commenced dock trails.
1500: Secured from dock trails.

11th June, Moored as before at repair dock at Lumbrum Point, Los Negros Island, Admiralty Islands.
0615: Ship underway for sea trails.
1823: Secured from sea trails and completed taking on fuel at fuel dock, anchored in (berth 252), Seedler Harbor, Manus Admiralty Islands.

12th June, Anchored as before in (berth 252).
0630: Underway, proceeding to net depot dock in Seedler Harbor, Manus, Admiralty Islands to take on cargo.
0643: Moored to net depot dock, commenced taking on cargo.
1700: Completed taking on cargo. (No description in log of what the cargo was).

13th June, Moored as before at net depot dock in Seedler Harbor, Manus, in the Admiralty Islands.

1232: Underway, proceeding independently to Manila Bay, Luzon, in the Philippine Islands.
1324: Passed entrance gate to Seedler Harbor, manus, Admiralty Islands, proceeding singly to Manila Bay, Luzon. Philippine Islands.

13th June to 22nd of June, Steaming singly as before. Proceeding to Manila Bay, Luzon. Philippine Islands.

22nd June
0940: Ship approaching inner Manila Bay, Luzon, Philippine Islands.
1037: Anchored in berth (40) in Manila Bay, Luzon. Philippine Islands.

23rd June, Anchored as before in (berth 40) in Manila Bay, Luzon. Philippine Islands. U.S.S. Auburn (AGC-10) is (SOPA).

24th June to 26th June, Anchored in (berth 40). U.S.S. Auburn (AGC-10) is (SOPA).

26th June
0715: Underway to shift anchorage to Cavite to unload cargo from Manus, Admiralty Islands. 1714: Anchored off Cavite in Canaloa Bay, Luzon, in the Philippine Islands.

27th June, Anchored as before in Canaloa Bay, Luzon, in the Philippine Islands.
1025: Unloading cargo completed.
1120: Underway, proceeding to new anchorage.
1205: Anchored in Manila Bay, Luzon, in the Philippine Islands.

28th June, Anchored as before in Manila Bay, Luzon, in the Philippine Islands. U.S.S. Auburn (AGC-10) is (SOPA).

29th June, Underway, proceeding singly to San Pedro Bay, Leyte Gulf, Leyte,in the Philippine Islands.

1st July 1945, Arrived at San Pedro Bay, Leyte Gulf, Leyte, in the

Philippine Islands.
1137: Anchored in San Pedro Bay, Leyte Gulf, Leyte, in the
Philippine Islands.

2nd July, Anchored as before in San Pedro bay, Leyte Gulf, Leyte, in
the Philippine Islands.
1054: Underway, proceeding to Guian Roadstead, Samar, in the
Philippine Islands.
1545: Anchored in Guian Roadstead, Samar, in the Philippine
Islands.

3rd July to 5th July, Anchored as before in Guian Roadstead, Samar,
Philippine Islands

0630: underway, proceeding to the RAN Kurumba (Australian oil
taker) to take on fuel.
1630: Moored alongside the RAN Kurumba to take on fuel.
1748: Underway from alongside the RAN Kurumba, taking on fuel
completed.
1758: Anchored in San Pedro Bay, Leyte Gulf, Leyte, in the
Philippine Islands.

6th July to 7th July, Anchored as before in San Pedro Bay, Leyte Gulf,
Leyte, in the Philippine Islands.
0857: Ship underway for Guian Roadstead, Samar, in the Philippine
Islands.
1625: Anchored in Guian Roadstead, Samar, in the Philippine
Islands.

8th July, Anchored as before.

9th July, Anchored as before. Worked on (A/T) net line. (No times in
log for work on net line or description of work).

10th July, Anchored as before in Guian Roadstead, Samar, Philippine
Islands.
0810: Underway for San Pedro Bay, Leyte Gulf, Leyte, in the

Philippine Islands.

1543: Anchored in San Pedro Bay, Leyte Gulf, Leyte, in the Philippine Island.

11th July, Anchored as before in San Pedro Bay, Leyte Gulf, Leyte, in the Philippine Islands.

0622: Underway to anchor and tie to dolphin west of Jinamol Island, for pulling pipeline from beach to dolphin.

0634: Moored to dolphin.

1600: Working on pulling pipeline from beach to dolphin.

2200: Completed pulling pipeline to dolphin.

12th July, Moored as before, to dolphin off Jinamol Island.

0637: Underway, at slow speed thru the Camoro Pudan Islands to pick up moorings. Have leadsman in the chains for sounding.

1007: Commenced operations on mooring buoy.

1036: Mooring buoy and anchor, recovered. Proceeding out from among the Camoro Pudan Islands.

1130: Out from among the Camoro Islands now proceeding out of San Pedro Bay, Leyte Gulf, Leyte, in the Philippine Islands for Guian Roadstead, Samar, in the Philippine Islands.

1550: Anchored in Guian Roadstead, Samar, in the Philippine Islands.

13th July, Anchored as before in Guian Roadstead, Samar, Philippine Islands.

1330: Underway, proceeding to (YFD-64).

1353: Moored alongside (YFD-64) to discharge cargo. (Buoy and anchor).

1418: Completed discharging cargo, underway to anchorage.

1535: Anchored in (berth 329) in Guian Roadstead, Samar. Philippine Islands.

14thJuly to 23rd July, Anchored as before in (berth 329) in Guian Roadstead, Samar. Philippine Islands.

23th July

1050: Ships motor launch had an accident.

Note:

Report of accident, at (1050) while approaching a net mooring buoy for the purpose of putting a line to said buoy, the ships motor launch in passing under the bow of the ship to receive the line. The motor launch was caught against the ships bow, causing the motor launch to capsize. The launch sank in (9) fathoms of water. Buoy set at location of accident for future salvage operations.

23rd July
1912: Anchored in Guian Roadstead, Samar. Philippine Islands.

24thJuly, Anchored in Guian Roadstead, Samar. Philippine Islands.
Note: Weather unfavorable for salvage operations on sunken motor launch.

25th July, Anchored as before.
0700: Underway to recover sunken motor launch.
0900: Anchored in area of sunken motor launch, commenced diving operations.
1010: Completed diving operations, motor launch recovered and placed on (LCM) then send ashore for repairs.

26th July to 29th July, Ship working on net line in Guian Roadstead, Samar. Philippine Islands.

29th July
1349: Underway, proceeding to Tacloban,
1957 anchored in San Pedo Bay, Leyte Gulf, in the Philippine Islands.

30th July, Anchored as before.
0830: Underway, proceeding out of San Pedro Bay en route to Balusao water hole.
0935: Moored alongside (PCE 875) to receive fresh water from beach at Balusao.
1118: Underway from alongside (PCE 875), completed taking on fresh water.

1522: Anchored in Guian Roadstead, Samar, in the Philippine Islands.

1ˢᵗAugust to 13ᵗ August, Working on (A/T) net line in Guian Roadstead, Samar, Philippine Islands.

13ᵗʰ August
1005: Completed work on (A/T) net line.
1136: Anchored in Guian Roadstead, Samar, in the Philippine Islands.
1525: Underay, to take on water at Balusao, Lauaan Bay, Samar, Philippine Islands.
1849: Moored alongside (YW-90) at Balusao, Lauaan Bay, Samar in the Philippine Islands.
1940: Completed taking on fresh water.

14ᵗʰ August, Moored as before alongside (YW-90) at Balusao, Lauaan Bay, Samar, in the Philippine Islands.
0600: Underway, proceeding to San Pedro Bay, Leyte Gulf, Leyte, in the Philippine Islands.
1308: Anchored near U.S.S. Rigel (AR-11) to effect necessary repairs to engines. In San Pedro Bay, Leyte Gulf, Leyte, in the Philippine Islands.

15ᵗʰ August, Anchored as before.
1010: Underway, proceeding to U.S.S. Yosemite (AD-19) in (berth 33) repairs.
1046: Moored alongside the U.S.S. Yosemite (AD-19) in (berth 33).
1104: (LCS-95) alongside.
1431: (LCS-95) underway from alongside.
1455: (LCS-87) alongside.
1515: (LCS-64) moored out board of (LCS-87).
1826: (LCS-64) underway from alongside (LCS-87).
1831: (LCD-87) underway from alongside

ON AUGUST 15ᵀᴴ, 1945, THE WAR IN THE PACIFIC IS OVER. ALL OVER THE WORLD THE PEOPLE WERE CELEBRATING THE END OF WORLD WAR 11.

16th August to 21st August, Moored as before alongside the U.S.S. Yosemite (AD-19) in (berth 33) in San Pedro Bay, Leyte Gulf, Leyte, in the Philippine Islands. U.S.S. Ocelot (IX-110) is (SOPA).

21stAugust
0755: Shifted berths.
0812: Anchored in San Pedro Bay, Leyte Gulf. Located in the Philippine Islands.

22nd August: Anchored as before in San Pedro Bay, Leyte Gulf, Leyte, in the Philippine Islands.

Note:
16thAugust
1900: The movies were being held on the forecastle and most of the personnel on board were at the movies. The movie was GILDA.

One of the sailors on board that was not at the movies but was writing a letter home. He had the radio on in the mess hall when the armed forces radio came on the air and said the war was over. He ran forward to tell the crew that the war was over. No one believed him, till every ship in the harbor started shooting off every gun that was on board. When things settled down in the harbor some ships had a few holes and damage that was not present at sun set.

When the news came on the day of the (17th), we found out that World War 11 ended on the 15th August. That an atomic bomb had been dropped on the 6th August, on a town called Hiroshima and then another atomic bomb was dropped on the (9th) August, on a town called Nagasake. Then on the 15th August, the Emperor of Japan unconditionally surrendered.

23rd August, Anchored as before.
1300: Underway, proceeding to Guian Roadsteed, Samara, in the Philippine Islands. With (LCVP) in tow.
1730: Anchored in Guian Roadsteed, Samara, in the Philippine Islands. No entry in log to what happen to (LCVP).

24th August to 25th August, Anchored as before.

1257: Underway, proceeding to Lauaan Bay, Samar, in the Philippine Islands.

1758: Anchored in Lauaan Bay, Samar, in the Philippine Islands.

1921: Underway to go alongside (YW 176) to take on fresh water.

1945: Moored alongside (YW 176).

1949 (YTL 316) came alongside.

2320: Completed taking on fresh water.

2343: (YTL 316) underway from alongside.

2346: Underway from alongside (YW 176), ship proceeding to anchorage in Lauaan Bay, Samar, in the Philippine Islands.

26th August, ship underway as before.

0015: Anchored in Lauaan Bay.

0703: Underway, proceeding to Guian Roadstead, Samar, in the Philippine Islands.

1037: Anchored in Guian Roadstead, Samar, in the Philippine Islands.

27th August, Anchored as before.

0707: Underway to pull barge off reef.

0739: Anchored, preparatory to pulling barge off reef.

0958: Salvage operations completed, underway to anchorage in Guian Roadstead, Samar, Philippine Islands. (No entry in log to what reef the barge was on).

28th August, Anchored as before.

0815: Underway to pull Coast Guard Cutter (83371) off reef. (371 represent the length of Cutter, 83 is the hull number).

0940: Pulled Coast Guard Cutter (83371) off the reef.

1110: Underway with Coast Guard Cutter (83371) alongside.

1206: Anchored in Guian Roadstead, Samar, in the Philippine Islands.

1218: Coast Guard Cutter (83371) underway from alongside.

29th August to 3rd September, Anchored as before in Guian Roadstead, Samar, in the Philippine Islands.

3rd September
1618: The U.S.S.Cinnamon (AN-50) came alongside.

Note:
On the 2ND of September 1945 Japan's formal surrendered on the
battleship the U.S.S. Missouri (BB-63) in Tokyo Bay, Japan.

4th September, Anchored as before in Guian Roadstead, Samar, in the
Philippine Islands.
0705: U.S.S. Cinnamon (AN-50) underway from alongside.
Underway, proceeding to disassemble net sections of net line in
Guian Roadstead, Samar, in the Philippine Islands.

4th September to 10th September, Working as before on disassembling
net sections in Guian Roadstead, Samar, in the Philippine Islands.

10th September
1205: Underway for Leyte Gulf, Philippine Islands searching for net
section reported adrift.
0918: Hoisted aboard drifting (SONO) buoy.
1445: Completed search for drifting new section, with negative
results in area between Manicani, Homonhon and Sulan Islands.
Anchored in Guian Roadstead, Samar, in the Philippine Islands.

11th September to 12th September, ship was working on net line

12th September
0827: The U.S.S Mango (AN-24) came alongside.
1030: U.S.S. Mango (AN-24) underway from alongside. (No entry in
log to way she was alongside).

13th September, Anchored in Guian Roadstead, Samar, In the
Philippine Islands.

0630: Underway, to northwest corner of Manicani Island to pull (YF
929) off reef.
1035: Tow cable carried away.

1630: Sent explosives shore to blast corral heads, obstructing free passage of barge.
2150: Pulled barge free of reef.
2220: Brought barge (YF 929) alongside.

2310: Underway, for new anchorage with (YF 929) alongside.
2325: Anchored off Manicani Island in the Philippine Islands.

14th September, Anchored as before.
0910: Underway for Guian Roadstead, Samar, in the Philippine Islands.
1039: Secured YF 929 to fleet mooring in Guian Roadstead, Samar, in the Philippine Islands.
1111: Moored alongside the U.S.S. Trinity (AO-13) to take on fuel.
1220: Completed taking on fuel, underway from alongside the U.S.S. Trinity (AO-13).
1558: Anchored in Guian Roadstead, Samar, in the Philippine Islands.

15th September to 22nd September, Anchored in Guian Roadstead, Samar, in the Philippine Islands.
1523: Underway and proceeding to (FYD-21).
1601: Entered dry dock (YFD-21), assisted by two (YTL's) tugs.
1637: Ship resting on keel blocks in dry dock (FYD-21).

23rd September to 2nd October, Resting on keel blocks in dry dock (FYD-21) along with (LST 245). (YFD-21) moored in Guian Roadstead, Samar, in the Philippine Islands. Ship in dry dock for repairs and cleaning of ships hull from water line to keel.

2nd October
1700: Commenced making preparations to leave dry dock (YFD-21).
1815: Underway out of dry dock (YFD-21).
1845: Anchored in Guian Roadstead, Samar, in the Philippine Islands.

7th October, Anchored as before.

0900: Underway to take on fresh water.

0920: Moored alongside the SS William H. Prescott a fresh water tanker.

0940: (YP-640) came alongside.

1455: (YP-640) underway from alongside.

1607: Completed taking on fresh water from the SS William H. Prescott. Ship underway from alongside and proceeding to anchorage.

1652: Anchored in Subic Bay, Luzon. In the Phillippine Islands.

October 8th to 22nd October, The ship was working on salvaging every other buoy attached to net section. Then towing section out to sea for disposal. U.S.S. Dobbin (AD-3) is (SOPA)

(Note: Death notice to all hands,

At (1025) on October 11th of 1945, death visited the U.S.S. Silverbell (AN51). For at this time at (1025) death came to Rudolph the ships mouse, (S/N) 100-00-00, USN. Rudolph first boarded this Navy ship at Mios Woendi Lagoon in the Schouten Islands off of Dutch New Guinea in August of 1944, being a sole survivor of some unknown vessel trying to make it to the beach on a piece of drift wood. Being spotted and rescued by the ships motor launch returning from the beach with supplies. He was brought on board and on the same day he was sworn in as ships mouse in August of 1944, with the rate of (Mouse 3rd class) and from all the joy he brought to the ship he rose rapidly up the ladder to (Mouse 1st class). Which was his rate at the time of his death.

He served valiantly as he went through the invasion of Leyte Gulf, Leyte, in the Philippine Islands. Doing his duties quietly and efficiently.

It is believed by the crew he is survived by countless brothers and sisters and also that his parents had passed away some time ago. The whereabouts of the survivors of his family are unknown.

Ships mouse Rudolph earned the Asiatic Pacific campaign ribbon with one bronze star, the Philippine Liberation ribbon with one bronze star and the American Campaign Medal. Rudolph was well liked aboard ship and many will mourn his passing. Death came quietly from natural causes. He is reaping his earned rewards at the happy hunting grounds in mouse heaven.

The burial will take place at 1300 with all hands present this day on the starboard side of the fantail. After the reading by the skipper, his body will be slid into the lagoon. After the service all hands back to ships routine.

16th October, Working net line as before.
0809: Underway to take on fresh water.
0825: Moored alongside water dock, commenced taking on fresh water.
0853: PCE-873 came alongside.
1018: Completed taking on fresh water.
1116: Underway, proceeding to Subic Bay, Luzon, in the Philippine Islands, to work on (A/T) nets.
1720: Anchored in Subic Bay, Luzon, in the Philippine Islands.

22nd October, Anchored as before.
0742: Underway top inner harbor to go alongside repair ship the U.S.S. Maui (ARG-18).
0915: Moored starboard side to U.S.S. Maui (ARG-8) with LSM-127 and LSM-30 in between.
0920: YMS-397 moored to our port side with YP-286 moored outboard. Working party from U.S.S. Maui (ARG-18) engaged in cleaning ships evaporators.
1645: YMS-397 and YP-286   underway from alongside.
1650: Underway, from alongside LSM-127 proceeding to Anchorage.
1748: Anchored in Subic Bay, Luzon, in the Philippine Islands.

23rd October, Anchored as before. U.S.S. Dobbin (AD-3) is (SOPA).

24th October, Anchored as before in Subic Bay, Luzon, in the Philippine Islands. The U.S.S. San Clemente (AG-79) is (SOPA)
0808: Underway, proceeding to water dock.
0952: Anchored off water dock.
1708: Underway to go alongside water dock.
1735: Moored alongside U.S.S. Teaberry (AN-34).

1750: Underway from alongside U.S.S. Teaberry (AN-34). (No entry in log why ship was alongside the U.S.S. Teaberry (AN-34).
1840: Moored alongside SS Mobile Bay (a fresh water tanker) to take on fresh water. (No entry for getting underway to go alongside tanker).
2200: completed taking on fresh water.

25th October, Moored as before alongside the SS Mobile Bay.
0755: Underway from alongside the SS Mobile Bay and proceeding to anchorage in Subic Bay, Luzon, In the Philippine Islands.

26th of October to 1st of November, Moored as before the U.S.S. Dobbin (AD-3) is (SOPA).

1st November
1125: Underway proceeding to Manila Bay, Luzon, in the Philippine Islands.
1820: Anchored in (berth 28), in the inner Harbor of Manila Bay, Luzon, in the Philippine Islands.

2nd November to 3rd of November, Anchored as before in Manila Bay, Luzon, in the Philippine Islands.

3rd November
1220: Underway, proceeding to go alongside of the U.S.S. Wildcat (AW-2)
1323: Moored alongside the YW-108 that is moored alongside the U.S.S. Wildcat (AW-2).
1420: Completed taking on fresh water. Underway proceeding to anchorage.
1455: Anchored in (berth 28) Manila Bay, Luzon, in the Philippine Islands.

4th November to 10th November, Anchored as before in (berth 28) Manila Bay, Luzon, in the Philippine Islands.

10th November

0925: Underway to shift berths.

1000: Anchored near SS Ocean Chief (SS fresh provision Ship) to take on fresh provisions.

1140: Completed taking on fresh provisions, underway proceeding to (berth 28) in Manila Bay, Luzon, Philippine Islands.

1210: Anchored in berth 28 in Manila Bay, Luzon, in the Philippine Islands. The U.S.S. San Clemente (AG-79) is (SOPA).

11th November to the 13th November, Anchored as before in (berth 28).

0849: Underway to calibrate compass.

1000: Calibrations completed.

1045: Moored to U.S.S. Panda (IX-125) to take on fuel.

1217: Completed taking on fuel, underway from alongside U.S.S. Panda (IX-125) proceeding to berth 28 in Manila Bay, Luzon. Philippine Islands.

1255: Anchored in (berth 28) in Manila Bay, Luzon, in the Philippine Islands. U.S.S. San Clemente (AG-79) is (SOPA).

14th November to 15th November, Anchored as before in (berth 28).

15th November

1050: on the 15th, underway out of Manila Bay, Luzon, in the Philippine Islands. Proceeding to Leyte Gulf, Luzon, in the Philippine Islands, to Guian Roadstead, Samar, in the Philippine Islands.

16th November to 18th of November, Steaming as before, proceeding to Guian Roadstead, Samar, in the Philippine Islands.

18th November

0700: Anchored in Guian Roadstead, Samar, in the Philippine islands.

1120: Underway to take on fresh water at small craft dock in Lauuan Bay, Samar, in the Philippine Islands

1500: Moored to small craft dock in Lauuan Bay, Samar, in the Philippine Islands. Commenced to take on fresh water.

1635: Completed taking on fresh water, underway proceeding to anchorage.

1708: Anchored in Lauuan Bay, Samar, In the Philippine Islands.

19th November, Anchored as before in Lauuan Bay, Samar, in the Philippine Islands.

0605: Underway, proceeding to Guian Roadstaead, Samar, in the Philippine Islands.

0915: Anchored in Guian Roadstead, Samar, in the Philippine Islands.

1500: Unfurled the homeward bound pennant from the pig stick. (At top of mast)

Note:

The homeward bound pennant is flown from the pig stick. By ships returning from extended overseas tours. The pennant is authorized for display by ships that have been on duty outside the limits of the United States continuously for at least 9 months. It is hoisted on getting under way for the United States and may be flown until sunset on day of arrival in port of destination. The pennant is similar to the commission pennant, but instead of the usual seven stars, there is one star for the first 9 months of overseas duty and one star for each additional 6 months. Total length of the pennant customarily is 1 foot for each officer and an enlisted member who served for a period in excess of 9 months. When the number of personnel produces an unwieldy pennant, the length of the pennant is restricted to the length of the ship. Upon arrival in a port of the United States, the blue portion containing the stars is presented to the commanding officer. The remainder of the pennant is divided equally among the officers and enlisted crew.

1500: Underway, proceeding to Enewetok Atoll, in the Marshall Islands in company with the U.S.S. Cinnamon (AN-50) and the U.S.S. Torchwood (AN-55).

19th November to 29th November, steaming in company as before with the U.S.S. Cinnamon (AN-50) and the U.S.S. Torchwood (AN-

55,) proceeding to Enewetok Atoll in the Marshall Islands.
1255: On the 29th of November anchored in berth (S-3) in Enewetok Atoll harbor in the Marshall Islands.

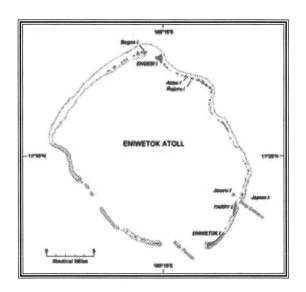

Eniwetok Atoll located in the Marshall Islands.

1456: Underway to go alongside (YO-83) for fuel.
1536: Moored alongside (YO-83), commenced taking on fuel.
1715: Completed taking on fuel, underway from alongside (YO-83) proceeding to (YO-187) to take on fresh water.
1740: Moored alongside (YO-187), commenced taking on fresh water.
1755: Completed taking on fresh water, underway proceeding to (berth S-3) in Enewetok Atoll harbor.
1820: Anchored in (berth S-3) in Enewetok Atoll harbor, in the Marshall Islands.

30th November, Anchored as before in (berth S-3) in Enewetok Atoll harbor, in the Marshall Islands.
1006: Underway, proceeding to Pearl Harbor, Oahu, Territory of Hawaii in company with U.S.S. Cinnamon (AN-50) and U.S.S. Torchwood (AN-55).

30th November to 9th December, Steaming in company as before with

U.S.S. Cinnamon (AN-50) and the U.S.S. Torchwood (AN-55).
Proceeding to Pearl Harbor, Oahu Island, in the Territory of Hawaii.

9th December, Steaming as before in company with U.S.S. Cinnamon (AN-50) and U.S.S. Torchwood (AN-55).

1110: Entering Pearl Harbor, Oahu Island, in the Territory of Hawaii.
1245: Moored to U.S.S. Cinnamon (AN-50) at dock ("V"6) with U.S.S. Torchwood (AN-55) alongside.

9th December to 12th December, Moored as before to U.S.S. Cinnamon (AN-50) and the U.S.S. Torchwood (AN-55) alongside.

12th December
0700:Underway, proceeding to San Francisco Bay, California, United States of America.
In company with U.S.S. Cinnamon (AN-50) and U.S.S. Torchwood (AN-55).

12th December to 21st December, Steaming in company with U.S.S. Cinnamon (AN-50) as OTC of Task Unit 182.1 and U.S.S. Torchwood (AN-55). Proceeding to San Francisco Bay, California, United States of America.

21st December: Steaming in company as before, with U.S.S. Cinnamon (AN-50) as (OTC) of (Task Unit 182.1) with the U.S.S. Torchwood (AN-55).

21 December
0650: The ships passed San Francisco light. Ship's entering San Francisco Bay still flying her homeward bound pennants.
0823: Passed under the Golden Gate Bridge over San Francisco Bay, California. The ships where meet at the Golden Gate Bridge by a large yacht loaded with young ladies waving and yelling, "welcome home" everyone. From the bridge they had signs hanging saying welcome home everyone and thanks for a great job well done.

The U.S.S. Silverbell (AN-51) left San Francisco Bay, California, on May 2nd 1944 and returned on December 21st of 1945 a total of 20+ months over seas.

0852: Anchored in anchorage #7.
0857: Ship inspected, ship given a clean bill by inspectors.
1950: tug came alongside for personnel being transferred.
1005: Tug underway from alongside with transferred personnel.
1313: Underway, proceeding to Naval Net Depot, Tiburon, California.

Sunset this day, 21st December 1945, the homeward bound pennant was lowered and the commissioning pennant was placed back on the pig stick and raised back in it's proper position on the mast.

21st December 1945, to the 7th of January 1946, Anchored as before off Naval Net Depot, Tiburon, California.

Note:
Christmas and New Years spent in San Francisco Bay.

7th January 1946,
1540: Ship underway as (CTU 06.12.2), in company with U.S.S. Cinnamon (AN-50) and U.S.S. Torchwood (AN-55) proceeding to San Pedro, California.

7th January to 9th of January: Steaming in company with U.S.S. Cinnamon (AN-50) and US.S. Torchwood (AN-55) with (OTC aboard the U.S.S. Silverbell (AN-51).

9th January
0732: Pilot came aboard at entrance to San Pedro Harbor to take ship to ("Y") anchorage.
0740: Entered San Pedro Harbor thru west entrance.
0755: Anchored in San Pedro Harbor in Berth ("Y").

9th January to16th January, Anchored as before in San Pedro Harbor in berth ("Y").

16th January
1340: Underway to go alongside the U.S.S. Cinnamon (AN-50).
1352: Moored alongside the U.S.S. Cinnamon (AN-50) in ("Y")
anchorage in San Pedro Harbor California.

16th January to 30th of January, Moored as before alongside the U.S.S.
Cinnamon (AN-50) in San Pedro Harbor.

30th of January, Tied up alongside the U.S.S. Cinnamon (AN-50) in
San Pedro Harbor.

0830: Commenced moving all ammunition from magazines to
main deck preparatory to off loading ammunition. Also make all
preparations to decommission the U.S.S. Silverbell (AN51).

1130: Underway from alongside the U.S.S. Cinnamon (AN-50),
proceeding to Naval Ammunition Depot at Seal Beach, California to
off load ammunition.
1415: Moored to (B-6 dock) at Naval Net and Ammunition Depot,
at Seal Beach, California.
1420: Commenced transferring ammunition.
1445: Completed transferring ammunition, underway, proceeding
out of Seal Beach, California to anchorage in Long Beach harbor,
Long Beach, California.
1550: Moored alongside the U.S.S. Cinnamon (AN-50) in ("Y")
anchorage in the inside mole of Long Beach harbor, Long Beach,
California.

30th January to 1st April, Moored as before, alongside the U.S.S.
Cinnamon (AN-50) in the inside mole of Long Beach harbor, Long
Beach, California. With the crew still at work decommissioning the
ship.

1st April
1020: Removed mooring lines from U.S.S. Cinnamon (AN-50) and

tug came alongside with pilot aboard.

1024: Underway for Naval Shipyard at Terminal island Long Beach, California.

1050: Moored alongside the U.S.S. Torchwood (AN-55) at (pier 3), (berth 32) Naval Shipyard, Terminal Island, Long Beach, California.

Note:

Stopped all decommissioning activity, commence putting the U.S.S. Silverbell (AN-51) back in commission. She is to return to the Pacific area for more salvage work in the Philippine Islands and other islands in the Pacific.

2nd April to 17th of April, moored as before alongside the U.S.S. Torchwood (AN-55) at (pier 3), (berth 32) at Naval Shipyard, Terminal Island, Long Beach, California.

17th April

1205: Underway from (pier 3) (berth 32) at the Naval Shipyard, Terminal Island, Proceeding to (Dry Dock #3) at naval Shipyard, Terminal Island, with the assistance of (YTB-400).

1246: Began flooding (dry dock #3).

1425: Ship resting on keel blocks in (dry dock #3) along with the U.S.S. Cliffrose (AN-42) in the Naval Shipyard, Terminal Island, Long Beach, California.

17th April to 29th April, Resting on keel blocks as before along with the U.S.S. Cliffrose (AN-42) in (dry dock #3) in the Naval Shipyard at Terminal Island, Long Beach, California.

29th April

1355: Ship became waterborne, flooding free of keel blocks in the (dry dock #3).

1610: Leaving (dry dock #3) with the assistance of (YTB-394) and (YTB-560).

1630: Pilot came aboard.

1640: Moored alongside the U.S.S. Cinnamon (AN-50) at (pier 2), (berth 23) Naval Shipyard, Terminal Island, Long Beach, California. 1705: LSM 231 came alongside (No entry why she was alongside or when she got underway from alongside).

30th April to 3rd May, Moored as before alongside the U.S.S. Cinnamon (AN-50) at (pier 2) (berth 23) Naval Shipyard, Terminal Island, Long Beach, California.

3rd May
1403: Pilot came aboard, Tugs (YTB-400) and (YTB-394) came alongside.
1415: With tugs (YTB-400) and (YTB-394) assisting in getting the U.S.S. Silverbell (AN-51) alongside the U.S.S. Cinnamon (AN-50) at (pier 2), (berth 23). Naval Shipyard, Terminal Island, Long Beach, California.
1423: Pilot left ship.
1425: Tugs cast off from alongside.

4th May to 21st May, Moored as before. Ship alongside the U.S.S. Cinnamon (AN-50) at (pier 2), (berth 23), Terminal Island, Long Beach, California.

21st May
0815: Underway from pier to let U.S.S. Cinnamon (AN-50) leave pier (2) with the assistance of Navy tug.
0836: Moored to pier 2, berth 23, Terminal Island, Long Beach, California.

22nd May to 1st of June, Moored as before to (pier 2), (berth 23), Terminal Island, Long Beach, California.
0820: 1st June, pilot came aboard.
0825: Underway for Cerritos Channel, Long Beach, California.
0925: Moored to pier (berth 2), in Cerritos Channel, Long Beach, California.
1055: U.S.S. Cinnamon (AN-50) came alongside.

2nd June to 5thJune, Moored as before at pier(berth 2), in Cerritos

Channel, Long Beach, California.

5th June
0835: The U.S.S. Cliffrose (AN-42) moored outboard U.S.S. Cinnamon (AN-50).

6th of June, The U.S.S. Torchwood (AN-55) moored outboard of the U.S.S. Cliffrose (AN-42).

6th June to 3rd July, Moored as before alongside pier (berth 2), in Cerritos Channel, Long Beach, California with U.S.S. Cinnamon (AN-50), U.S.S. Cliffrose (AN-42) and the U.S.S. Torchwood (AN-55) alongside.

Note: All work completed on U.S.S. Silverbell (AN-51). The ship and is ready for sea.

3rd July
1055: Underway, proceeding to Pearl Harbor, Territory of Hawaii in company with the U.S.S. Cinnamon (AN-50), the U.S.S. Torchwood (AN-55) and the U.S.S. Cliffrose (AN-42) and the (AN 42) is (OTC).

(4th of July), Steaming in company as before proceeding to Pearl Harbor, Territory of Hawaii, with the U.S.S. Cinnamon (AN-50), U.S.S. Cliffrose (AN-42) and the U.S.S. Torchwood (AN-55). 2220: U.S.S. Cinnamon (AN-50) dropped out of formation due to engine trouble.

5th July: Steaming in company as before proceeding to Pearl Harbor, Territory of Hawaii. The U.S.S. Torchwood (AN-55) left formation with the U.S.S. Cinnamon (AN-50) in tow returning to San Pedro, California.

6th July to 13th of July, Steaming in company with U.S.S. Cliffrose (AN-42) proceeding to Pearl Harbor, Territory of Hawaii. (OTC) is the U.S.S. Cliffrose (AN-42)).

1933: 13th of July, sighted the U.S.S. Torchwood (AN-55) distances 13 miles.
2205: U.S.S. Torchwood (AN-55) back in formation.

13th July to 16th July, Steaming in company as before.

16th July
0825: Passed (Able#1 buoy) at entrance to Pearl Harbor, Territory of Hawaii.
0900: Moored to dock at Hickam Field wharf, Pearl Harbor, Territory of Hawaii.

16th July to 16th August, Moored as before at Hickam Field wharf, Pearl Harbor, Territory of Hawaii

16th August
1300: Underway from alongside the wharf, at Hickam Field, Pearl Habor,Territory of Hawaii for Enewetok Atoll, in the Marshall Islands in company with U.S.S. Cliffrose (AN-42 as (OTC).

16th August to 22nd August, Steaming in company as before, proceeding to Enewetok Atoll, in the Marshall Islands.
(Note: Some time between the 22nd of August to the 24th of August our steaming orders were changed to go directly to Guam, in the Marianas Islands).

24th August
CROSSED THE INTERNATIONAL DATE LINE.

24th August to 3rd September, Steaming as before in company with the U.S.S. Cliffrose (AN-42) (OTC) is the U.S.S. Cliffrose (AN-42). Proceeding to Guam, in the Marianas Islands.

3rd September, Steaming in company as before with the U.S.S. Cliffrose as (OTC). Proceeding to Guam, Marianas Islands.
0843: Entered Apra Harbor, Guam, in the Marianas Islands.
0900: Moored alongside the U.S.S. Cliffrose (AN-42) in (berth 305),

in Apra Harbor, Guam, in the Marianas Islands.

4th September, Moored as before alongside the U.S.S. Cliffrose (AN-42) in (berth 305).
1230: U.S.S. Mango (AN-24) moored alongside.

5th September, Moored as before in (berth 305) alongside the U.S.S. Cliffrose (AN-42) with the U.S.S. Mango (AN-24) alongside.

6th September to 8th September, Moored in (berth 305) with the U.S.S. Cliffrose (AN-42) and U.S.S. Mango (AN-24 alongside.

8th of September:
0800: Underway, proceeding to Subic Bay, Luzon. Philippine Islands. In company with the U.S.S. Torchwood (AN-55) and the U.S.S. Cliffrose (AN-42) as (OTC).

9th September to 14th September, Steaming as before in company with Torchwood (AN-55) and the U.S.S. Cliffrose (AN-42) as (OTC)

14th September
2100: Entered Subic Bay, Luzon. Philippine Islands.
2158: Anchored in (berth 112), in Subic Bay, Luzon. Philippine Islands.

15th September to 20th September, Anchored as before in berth (112), in Subic Bay, Luzon, Philippine Islands.

20th of September
1344: Underway to assist (LST 574).
1430: Anchored off Cabangan Point.
1515: The (LCM) commenced pulling tow cable to (LST 574).
1620: Secured tow cable to (LST 574).

21st September, Anchored as before off Cabangan Point with tow cable secured to (LST 574).
0436: Ship underway with (LST 574) in tow, to Subic Bay, Luzon.

Philippine Islands. Proceeding to (berth 1), in Subic Bay, Luzon. Philippine Islands.

22nd September to 24th September, Anchored in (berth 1), in Subic Bay, Luzon, Philippine Islands. Assisted (LST 403), (LST 373) and (LST 315) in salvage work. (No entry in log of what kind of salvage word or what kind of assistance we gave to (LST 403, 373) and (LST 315).

24th September
1157: Ceased salvage operations, underway for (berth 13), Subic Bay, Luzon. Philippine Islands. (No entry to what kind of salvage work was being done).

25th September 28th September Ship in salvage operations. Subic Bay, Luzon, in the Philippine Islands. (No entry to what kind of salvage work).

28th September, Anchored in (berth 90), Subic Bay, Luzon. Philippine Islands. (No entry in log when the ship completed salvage operation, or when she moved to (berth 90).
1710: Underway, proceeding to the U.S.S. Passumpic (AO-107) to take on fuel.
1750: Moored alongside the U.S.S. Passumpic (AO-107) in (berth 170).

29th September: Moored as before alongside the U.S.S. Passumpic (AO-107) in (berth 170).
0733: Completed taking on fuel, underway proceeding to water dock.
1140: Moored to water dock, Subic Bay.
1305: U.S.S. Nimble (AM-266) came alongside.
1333: U.S.S. Phanton (AM-273) came alongside.
1732: to 1738: The U.S.S. Nimble (AM-266) and U.S.S. Phanton (AM-273) underway from alongside.
1743: Ship underway from water dock, proceeding to (berth 114).
1805: Anchored in (berth 114), Subic Bay, Luzon. Philippine Islands.

30th September, Anchored as before in (berth 114), Subic Bay, Luzon. Philippine Islands.
1508: Underway, proceeding to (berth 102).
1553: Anchored in (berth 102), Subic Bay, Luzon. Philippine Islands.

30th September to 7th of October, Anchored as before in berth 102, Subic Bay, Luzon. Philippine Islands.

7th October
1700: Proceeding to Maritan Point water dock.
1830: Moored alongside the U.S.C.G.C. Orchid (WAGL-240) at Maritan Point water dock.

8th October, Moored as before alongside the U.S.C.G.C. Orchid (WAGL-240) and Maritan Point water dock.
0555: Completed taking on fresh water, underway and proceeding to anchorage.
0620: Anchored in (berth 115), Subic Bay, Luzon. Philippine Islands.

9th October to 15th October, Set typhoon condition (2) and worked on salvage operations. (No entry in log of what kind of salvage operations).

15th October
1245: Ship underway to new anchorage.
1600: Anchored in berth (2), Subic Bay, Luzon. Philippine Islands.

16th October, Anchored as before in (berth 2), Subic Bay, Luzon. Philippine Islands
1035: Secured tow wire to (LST-46). (No entry in log to what happened to (LST-46) or when ship shifted to (berth 1), Subic Bay, Luzon. Philippine Islands.

17th October, Anchored in berth (1), Subic Bay, Luzon. Philippine Islands.
0050: Underway to commence salvage operations.
0113: Chain parted on tow cable.

0120: Anchored in (berth 7), Subic Bay, Luzon. Philippine Islands.
0920: Underway, proceeding to (berth 1).
0944: Anchored in (berth 1), Subic Bay, Luzon. Philippine Islands. Tow wire from ship out to (LSM-278). (No entry in log of what kind of salvage operations the ship was conducting).

18th October, Anchored in (berth 1), Subic Bay, Luzon. Philippine Islands. Tow cable out to (LSM-278).
0145: Underway to commence salvage operations. (No log entry to what kind of salvage operation). (No log entry to what happened to (LSM-278).
1630: Completed salvage operations, anchored in (berth 1), Subic Bay, Luzon. Philippine Islands. No entry why Stern wire out to (LSM-292). (No Description of salvage operations in log)

19th October, Anchored as before in (berth 1), Subic Bay, Luzon. Philippine Islands. No log entry to what happened to (LSM-292).
0215: Underway to commence salvage operations.
0305: Commence salvage operations. No description of salvage operations.
0340: Ceased salvage operations, proceeding to (berth 116).
0550: Anchored in (berth 116), Subic Bay, Luzon. Philippine Islands.

20th October, Anchored as before in (berth 116), Subic Bay, Luzon. Philippine Islands.
0910: Underway, proceeding to Maritan Point water dock.
0950: Moored alongside (LST-578), at water dock, commence taking on fresh water.
1240: Completed taking on fresh water, underway from alongside (LST-548) proceeding to (ARD-19).
1300: Moored alongside (ARD-19), commenced to pumping oil to (ARD-19).
1705: Completed pumping oil to (ARD-19), underway, proceeding to (berth 116), Subic Bay, Luzon. Philippine Islands.
1730: Anchored in (berth 116), Subic Bay, Luzon. Philippine Islands.

21st October to 24th of October, anchored in (berth 116), Subic Bay,

Luzon. Philippine Islands.

24th of October
0630: Got underway for Manila Bay, Luzon, in the Philippine Islands.
1313: Entered Manila Bay, Luzon, In the Philippine Islands.
1345: Anchored in (berth 33), Manila Bay, in the Philippine Islands.

25th October to 28th October, Anchored as before in (berth 33), Manila Bay, Luzon, Philippine Island. U.S.S. Taluga (AO-62) is (SOPA).

28th of October:
0703: Underway, proceeding to Subic Bay.
1228: Entered Subic Bay, proceeding to water dock at Maritan Point.
1320: Moored alongside (W-240) at water dock at Maritan Point, Subic Bay, Luzon, in the Philippine Islands.
1533: Completed taking on fresh water, underway proceeding to (500) yards North of (berth 206), Subic Bay, Luzon, in the Philippine Islands.
(No time in log to when ship anchored in (berth 206).

29th October, Anchored as before in (berth 206), Subic Bay.
1045: Underway proceeding in accordance with instructions from Port Director. (No entry in log as to what kind of instructions).
1115: Commenced scheduled operations.
1615: Completed scheduled operations. Anchored in (berth 12), Subic Bay.

30th October to 4th November, Anchored as before in various berths in, Subic Bay. Working at various scheduled operations. (No log entry or description of various operations).

4th November, Anchored (500) yards North of (berth 206), Subic Bay, Luzon, in the Philippine Islands.
1602: Underway, proceeding to (YMS-2017) to put out fire.
1615: Anchored (200) yards from (YMS-2017).

1645: Underway for anchorage, that is about (100) yards North of (berth 206), Subic Bay, Luzon, in the Philippine Islands.
1705: Anchored (100) yards North of (berth 206), Subic Bay, Luzon, in the Philippine Islands.

5th November, Anchored as before (100) yards North of (berth 206), Subic Bay, Luzon, in the Philippine Islands.
1000: Underway, proceeding to Maritan Point water dock, Subic Bay, Luzon, in the Philippine Islands.
1100: Moored alongside (PGM -20) (a patrol vessel, motor gun boat) at Maritan Point water dock, Subic Bay, Luzon, in the Philippine Islands to take on fresh water.
1300: Completed taking on fresh water, underway for buoy tending operations.
1350: Picked up (buoy "R") to clear riser.
1410: Riser cleared, lowered buoy ("R").
1455: Underway, proceeding to U.S.S. Cliffrose (AN-42) in (berth 116), Subic Bay, Luzon, in the Philippine Islands.
1545: Moored alongside the U.S.S. Cliffrose (AN-42) in (berth 116), Subic Bay, Luzon, in the Philippine Islands.

6th November, Moored as before alongside the U.S.S. Cliffrose (AN-42) in (berth 116), Subic Bay, Luzon, Philippine Islands.
0653: Underway from alongside the U.S.S. Cliffrose (AN-42) to commence buoy tending operations.
1134: Completed clearing raiser of mooring buoy (at berth 208).
1140: Ship underway for anchorage.
1150: Anchored (200) yards North of (berth 208), Subic Bay, Luzon, in the Philippine Islands.

7th November to 11th of November, Anchored as before (200) yards North of (berth 208), Subic Bay, Luzon, Philippine Islands.

11th of November
1308: Underway, proceeding to Subic City area to hook up tow wire to (LST-46).
1430: Completed passing tow wire to (LST-46).

12th November, Anchored as before off Apalit Point, Subic Bay, Luzon, in the Philippine Islands. With tow wire secured to (LST-46). 1525: Switched tow wire from (LST-46) to (LST-596).

13th November, Underway towing (LST-596).
0200: Anchored in (berth 6), Subic Bay, Luzon, in the Philippine Islands. Tow wire secured to (LST-596).
0800: Cast off (LST-596) underway proceeding to Maritan point water dock, Subic Bay, Luzon, in the Philippine Islands.
0930: Moored alongside Maritan Point water dock, Subic Bay, Luzon, in the Philippine Islands to take on fresh water.
1306: Completed taking on fresh water, underway from alongside water dock, proceeding to vicinity of Apalit Point, Subic Bay.
1355: Anchored in vicinity of Apalit Point, Subic Bay, Luzon, in the Philippine Islands.
1500: Secured tow wire to (LST-894).

14th November, Anchored as before in vicinity of Apalit Point, Subic Bay Luzon, in the Phiippine Islands. Tow wire secured to (LST-894).
0001: Ship underway with (LST-894) in tow.
0005: Cast off (LST-894), underway for anchorage.
0125: Anchored in (berth 116), Subic Bay, Luzon, in the Philippine Islands.
1320: Underway, proceeding to vicinity of Requena Island, Subic Bay, in the Philippine Islands.
1600: Secured tow wire to U.S.S. Villalobos (IX-145).

15th November, Anchored as before in (berth 39), Subic Bay, Luzon, in the Philippine Islands. With tow wire secured to U.S.S. Villalobos (IX-145).
0300: Took strain on tow wire secured to U.S.S. Villalobos (IX-145).
0115: U.S.S. Cliffrose (AN-42), moored alongside.
0120: Cast off tow wire to U.S.S. Villalobos (IX-145). The Villalobos (IX-145) underway on her own power.
0208: U.S.S. Cliffrose (AN-42), underway from alongside.
0215: Underway, proceeding to (berth 206), Subic Bay, Luzon, in the Philippine Islands.

0240: Anchored in (berth 206), Subic Bay, Luzon, in the Philippine Islands.
16th November to 19th November anchored in (berth 206), Subic Bay, Luzon, in the Philippine Islands.

19th November
1740: (YTB-495) came alongside with (YTL-621) in tow, secured (YTL-621) alongside, (YTB-495) underway from alongside (YTL-621).
1800: underway, with (YTL-621) in tow, proceeding to Cavite Navy Base, Manila, in the Philippine Islands.

20th November, Steaming independently, proceeding to Cavite Navy Base, Manila in the Philippine Islands.
0600: Entered Cavite Navy Base (yard), Manila in the Philippine Islands.
0620: Ship anchored off, Cavite Navy Base (yard), Manila, in the Philippine Islands.
0955: Anchored (YTL-621) off Cavite Navy Base (yard), Manila, in the Philippine Islands. Ship underway, proceeding back to Subic Bay, Luzon, in the Philippine Islands.
1505: Entered Subic Bay, Luzon, in the Philippine Islands. Underway to Maritan Point water dock.
1602: Moored alongside water dock at Maritan Point, Subic Bay, in the Philippine Islands.
1805: Completed taking on fresh water, proceeding to anchorage.
1817: Anchored in berth (207), Subic Bay, Luzon, in the Philippine Islands.

21st November to 23rd November anchored in (berth 207), Subic Bay, Luzon, in the Philippine Islands.

23rd November
2131: Underway to take (PGM -19) in tow and place her alongside the Alava dock.
2225: Underway with (PGM-19) alongside.
2345: (PGM-19) moored alongside Alave dock.

2355: Ship underway from alongside (PGM-19), proceeding to (berth 207).

24th November to 3rd December anchored in (berth 207), Subic Bay, Luzon, in the Philippine Islands.

3rd December:
0539: Underway, proceeding to the vicinity of (berth 73) to assist U.S.S. Elder (AN-20) in taking (LST-1056) to (ARD-19).
0645: Moored alongside (LST-1056).
0715: Underway with (LST-1056) alongside, proceeding to (ARD-19).
0915: All ships lines free of (LST-1056). (LST-1056) moored alongside (ARD-19). Ship proceeding to (berth 207), Subic Bay, Luzon, in the Philippine Islands.
0925: Anchored in (berth 207), Subic Bay, Luzon, Philippine Islands.

4th December, Anchored as before in (berth 207), Subic Bay, Luzon, in the Philippine Islands.
1305: Ship underway for Alava dock, Subic Bay, Luzon, in the Philippine Islands.
1323: Moored to (YO-8) at Alava dock.
1335: Underway with (YO-8) alongside.
1353: (YO-8) anchored in (berth 207).
1355: Underway from alongside (YO-8). Proceeding to (PGM-19) at Alava dock.
1415: Moored alongside (PGM-19) at Alave dock.
1423: Underway from Alava dock with (PGM-19) alongside.
1435: Moored (PGM-19) alongside Alava dock, (No log entry to why (PGM-19) was moved).
1445: Underway from alongside (PGM-19). Ship proceeding to (berth 207), Subic Bay, Luzon, in the Philippine Islands.
1455: Anchored in (berth 207), Subic Bay, Luzon, in the Philippine Islands.

5th December, Anchored as before in (berth 207), Subic Bay, Luzon, in the Philippine Islands.

0830: Underway in accordance with port Directors Dispatch (#042327Z) to put (LSM-171) alongside Alava dock Subic Bay, Luzon, in the Philippine Islands.

0955: Took (LSM-171) alongside for towing.

1125: Cast off (LSM-171) at Alava dock, proceeding to water dock at Maritan Point, Subic Bay, Luzon, in the Philippine Islands.

1205: Moored alongside water dock at Maritan Point, Subic Bay, Luzon, in the Philippine Islands.

1332: Completed taking on fresh water, underway to (berth 207).

1350: Anchored in (berth 207), Subic Bay, Luzon, in the Philippine Islands.

6th December to 9th December, Anchored as before in berth (207), in Subic Bay, Luzon, in the Philippine Islands.

9th December

1022: Underway, proceeding to fuel pier.

1105: Moored to fuel pier, commence taking on fuel.

1418: Completed taking on fuel, underway, proceeding to Alava dock to fuel U.S.S. Buckeye (AN-13).

1503: Moored alongside (LCI-421).

1558: Commenced discharging fuel to the U.S.S. Buckeye (AN-13).

1915: Completed transferring fuel to the U.S.S. Buckeye (AN-13).

10th December, Moored as before as out board ship to the U.S.S. Buckeye (AN-13), (LCI-371) (LCI-397, LCI-421) at Alava dock, Subic Bay, Luzon, Philippine Islands.

1253: Underway from alongside (LCI-421), ship proceeding to Paniocan Point.

1515: Moored alongside the U.S.S. Elder (AN-20).

1600: Secured tow cable to the U.S.S. Orvetta (IX-147).

2130:Commence salvage operations. (No log entry what kind of salvage operations was performed or what happened to U.S.S. Orvetta (IX-147).

2345: Anchored 200 yards North of (berth 206), Subic Bay,Luzon, in the Philippine Islands.

11th December, Anchored as before in (berth 206), Subic Bay, Luzon, in the Philippine Islands.

1435: Underway, proceeding to the U.S.S. Elder (AN-20).

1500: Moored alongside the U.S.S. Elder (AN-20).

1538: Passed tow cable to (YF-1040).

2230: Commenced towing operations.

2325: Took YF-1040 alongside, cast off U.S.S. Elders (AN-20) tow cable.

2355: Underway, proceeding to anchorage with (YF-1040) in tow alongside.

12th December Underway with (YF-1040) in tow alongside. Proceeding to (berth 206), Subic Bay, Luzon, in the Philippine Islands.

0010: Anchored (500) yards North of (berth 206).

0755: (YF-1040) underway from alongside, in tow by two small craft, (LSM) and a (LCVP).

1315: Underway, proceeding to Subic City.

1540: Moored alongside the U.S.S. Cliffrose (AN-42) (500) yards south of Apalit Point.

1745: Secured stern tow cable to the U.S.S. Elder (AN-20).

2240: Underway to commence salvage operations.

2325: Commenced salvage operations.

2340: Ceased salvage operations, underway for anchorage. (No log entry to what kind of salvage operations or what happened to the U.S.S. Elder (AN-20).

13th December: Anchored North of (berth 207), Subic Bay.

14th December, Moored alongside PGM-19 in a nest consisting of U.S.S. Advantage and YW-123 at Alava dock, Subic Bay. (No entry in log when ship got underway for Alava dock).

0905: Underway, proceeding to anchorage.

0915: Anchored North of (berth 207), Subic Bay, Luzon, in the Philippine Islands.

15th December to 17th December, Anchored as before, north of (berth

207), Subic Bay.

0805: Underway, proceeding to fuel jetty.

0925: Moored alongside fuel jetty, commenced to take on fuel.

1245: Completed taking on fuel, underway from fuel jetty and proceeding to berth at Alava dock.

1343: Moored alongside U.S.S. Bolster (ARS-38) out board of (PCE-886) at Alava dock.

1440: Underway, from alongside U.S.S. Bolster (ARS-38) to salvage operations on SS Ryder Hanify.

1511: Anchored in (berth 201).

1515: Passed tow cable to SS Ryder Hanify.

1517: Commence towing operations of SS Ryder Hanify.

1655: Secured from salvage operations. (No entry in ships log when tow cable was disconnected from the SS Ryder Hanify or what happened to her). Ship underway to take on water at Maritan Point, Subic Bay, Luzon, in the Philippine Islands.

1740: Moored alongside U.S.S. Elder (AN-20) at water dock, Maritan Point, Subic Bay, Luzon in the Philippine Islands.

18th December, Moored as before alongside U.S.S. Elder (AN-20) at Maritan Point water dock.

0645: Underway, proceeding to anchorage.

0700: Anchored in (berth 207), Subic Bay, Luzon, in the Philippine Islands.

19th December, Anchored as before in (berth 207), Subic Bay, Luzon, in the Philippine Islands.

20th December, Anchored as before in (berth 207), Subic Bay, Luzon, in the Philippine Islands.

1516: Underway and out of Subic Bay, Luzon, in the Philippine Islands In route to Shanghai, China. In company with U.S.S. Cliffrose (AN-42)

21st December: Steaming as before in company with U.S.S. Cliffrose (AN-42).

1113: U.S.S. Cliffrose (AN-42) broke down.

1215: Took U.S.S. Cliffrose (AN-42) in tow and proceeded back to Subic Bay, Luzon, in the Philippine Islands.

22nd December: Steaming as before with U.S.S. Cliffrose in tow, proceeding back to Subic Bay, Luzon, in the Philippine Islands.
2252: Entered Subic Bay, Luzon, in the Philippine Islands. With U.S.S. Cliffrose in tow, proceeding to Alava dock.
2340: Cast off tow cable to U.S.S. Cliffrose (AN-42).
2355: Moored alongside U.S.S. Cliffrose (AN-42).

23rd December, Moored alongside U.S.S. Cliffrose (AN-42).
0130: Moored U.S.S. Cliffrose (AN-42) alongside (LST-598) at Alava dock, Subic Bay, Luzon, in the Philippine Islands.

0145: Underway from alongside U.S.S. Cliffrose (AN-42). Ship underway out of Subic Bay, Luzon, in the Philippine Islands in route to Shanghi, China.

23rd December to the 28th December: Steaming independently in route to Shanghi, China.

December 25th 1946 (Christmas) was spent at sea between Subic Bay and Shanghai China.

28th December
1212: Sighted the Yangtze entrance light to the Yangtze River.
1320: Took station astern of pilot vessel, proceeding up the Yangtze River.

1815: Anchored in the Yangtze River in the Quarantine anchorage.

29th December, Anchored as before in the Quarantine anchorage, Yangtze River.

1218: Pilot came aboard.
1258: Underway down the Yangtze River to the Wangpoo River, down the Wangpoo River to Shanghai, China.

1458: Moored alongside Wayside Wharf, Naval Operating Base Shanghai, China.

New Years Eve, spent tied to a dock in Shanghai China. (January 1ˢᵗ 1947 came on board the Silverbell with little fan fare).

29ᵗʰ December to 10ᵗʰ January 1947, Moored as before alongside Wayside Wharf, Naval Operating Base Shanghai, China.
29ᵗʰ December to 10ᵗʰ January, The following ships came alongside: (YW-90, YTB-520 and YTB-518).
1ˢᵗ January 1947, U.S.S. Cliffrose (AN-42) came alongside.

10ᵗʰ January
0955: The U.S.S. Cliffrose (AN 42) got underway from alongside.
1340 Ship underway, proceeding to buoy (17-A).
1408: Moored alongside U.S.S. Cliffrose (AN-42) at buoy (17-A).

10th January
1420: Secured the main engines for the last time moored to buoy (17-A).
1435: Decommissioned ship in accordance with dispatch (#190118Z) received in December 1946. The dispatch is from Commander Naval Forces Philippines. Secured all auxiliaries. Then the U.S.S. Silverbell (AN51) was transferred to the Chinese Maritime Customs for use as a buoy and lighthouse tender.

Note:
    While on active duty, (191) ships came along side the Silverbell to off load fuel or water or for repairs of all kinds.
28ᵗʰ January 1947 the Silverbell AN51 was struck from the United States Navy's inventory.

This finishes the story of just one of the little ships that did her job and to help bring the war to a close.

Now starts the last part of the story about the silver recovery in Caballo Bay.

The first Navy ship to arrive in Manila Bay to start the next phase of the silver recovery is the U.S.S. Teak (AN-35) and the ship is attached to (Ship Salvage, Fire Fighting and Rescue Unit, Service Force, Pacific) with (Lt.) Byron Pierce Hollett commanding.

U.S.S. Teak (AN-35)

Arriving on June 16th of 1945, near the location of the sunken treasure. The Teak with her ships crew and Navy divers and Army divers from the Corp of Engineers and a Navy prisoner of war that had helped in dumping the silver in Manila Bay. He was indeed generous in taking the time to help, for he had been a prisoner of war for approximately (3 ½) years and was anxious to go home. From the bearing he could remember will be the approximate location for a starting point for the Teak.

Now from this point a large square area of Manila Bay between Corregidor and Caballo island was laid out with a buoy and a concrete clump to hold the buoy in place, this was done at all corners of the grid.

Anchoring the Teak at the starting point from the bearing points which are Corregidor light, the highest point on Caballo Island, the highest point on Malinta hill on (Corregidor) and the East end of Fort Drum. Then at (1400) on the same day they began searching for the silver treasure from the bearings and then securing the operations at (1640) with no treasure found.

Finding nothing on the dives could be that the operation of dumping the silver at night and with the condition of the boats drifting with the current, all bearings could be off some distances from where the silver actually settled on the bottom of the bay.

The Teak continues the same operation on the 17th and the 18th of June with no luck in finding the silver pesos.

On the 16th, 17th and the 18th the divers in their effort to locate the treasure on the bottom of Caballo Bay had a extremely hard time seeing due to the thick layer of silt on the bay floor.

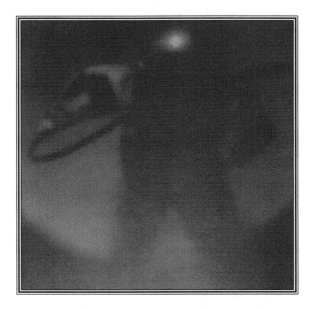

The silt makes for bad visibility

This silt is from the Pasig River that empties into Manila Bay and is carried from the mouth of the river through Manila Bay and Caballo Bay then out to the South China Sea. The silt has been deposited on the bay floor for many years, so at every step the divers took it disturbed the silt so bad it makes the visibility to see almost impossible.

The visibility problem is somewhat solved by placing a concrete clump on the bay floor with a vertical line going to a marker buoy on the surface. Then a horizontal line was attached to the vertical line at (10-foot) intervals a knot was placed all the way to the end of the horizontal line. So at each (10-foot) interval the diver would make a (360 degree) sweep of the area till he reached the end of the line. Finding nothing on the sweep the concrete clump was moved to a new location and the same procedure was started all over again.

The captain of the Teak decided against using the divers for a while due to the bad visibility. He had worked out a plan using a (55) gallon oil drum as a large sieve. Then burning a lot of holes in the drum and dragging it along the bottom of the bay in hopes of picking up some silver coins.

The process was very slow, and went on for a while crisscrossing the area where the silver was though to be. Every so often the drum would be brought to the surface and the contents dumped on deck, hoping to find some silver coins in the mud and other debris brought up from the bottom.

After several weeks of searching a few silver pesos were retrieved from the oil drum when it's contents were dumped on deck. The area where the few coins were picked up, was thoroughly searched, dragging the oil drum back and forth until one load, was dumped on deck which was loaded with silver coins. A location buoy was lowered to mark the location of the silver.

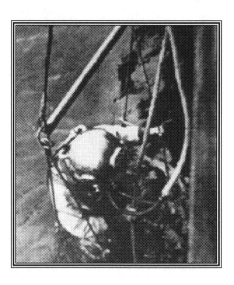

Putting diver over the side from the USS Teak (AN-35).

Then on 19th of June the Captain of the Teak positioned a rectangular mooring site with anchor buoys at all four corners and then using the four buoys to hold the ship in position by mooring cables to each buoy from port and starboard sides of the bow and stern so the ship could not swing but stay in one position. (If a ship is anchored with either port or starboard anchors she will most likely swing with the wind and make diving difficult). With this four point system the ship will stay in one position. Then on the morning of the 20th of June the ship went to general quarters. The Teak got underway for a harbor off Corregidor. After securing from general quarters, the ship got under way at (1340) for the salvage site. At (1420) arriving at the site she moored to the four mooring buoys in Caballo Bay. The diving operations started at (1530) and at (1605) the first silver pesos are found in (15.5) fathoms of water.

(T-5) Edward Smith (Army Corp of Engineers) instructing
divers from the U.S.S. Teak (AN-35)

Loose silver before bagging on the decks of the USS Teak (AN-35)

On the 21st of June in Caballo Bay The U.S.S. Teak starts diving operation at (0846) where the silver was finally located. At (1630) on the same day the first full (55) gallon ("G.I.") can of silver pesos was brought to the surface and hoisted aboard. From that day on the diving continued except at times the ship had to move to new anchorages in inner harbor of Manila for water, fuel, supplies or bad weather and heavy seas. Also while in the inner harbor she picked up a new member of the crew or transferred a member of the crew to the beach. Also the work was interrupted at times by small craft coming alongside with armed guards to pick up recovered silver pesos. The small craft then transports the silver to the beach where it is counted again and put in security.

Army diver T/Sgt Harrison T. Martin with the Corp of Engineers,
looking at the silver he found on the bottom of Caballo Bay

There were different kinds of interruptions, this ship had in the recovery process of the silver pesos, bad weather, high seas, fresh water, fuel, personnel changes, small craft alongside to pick silver cargo and that is what changes the plan of the day. Another case in point was on 12th of August 1945, when Army diver (S/Sgt) James B. Crosby was taken to Manila with a mild case of the bends. Also the interruption on (14th August 1945), when Japan's unconditional surrender, to end World War 11 in the Pacific.

Navy diver Sam Black in standard diving gear on a diving platform,
on his way to the bottom of Caballo Bay

The silver operation went on with many of the interruptions till September 12th, 1945 when all hands to quarters at (1300) for (Lt) Walter C. Hale USN/R to relieve (Lt) Byron P. Hollett USN/R as commanding officer of the U.S.S. Teak.

Virgil Cole (CM2c) having some pleasant dreams on $ 100,000 of silver pesos on the deck of the USS Teak (AN-35)

As of the September 13th the silver recovery was back in operation under the command of (Lt) W.C. Hale. With a Army officer on board as security officer to watch over the recovered silver on verbal orders from the Provost Marshall and the Commander of Salvage Group Philippine Sea Frontier. All conditions stayed pretty much the same as before the weather, fuel, water, and the change of personnel and the diving operations. No entry was made when (Lt) Hale was promoted to (Lt Cdr).

12th November 1945
0630: Ship got underway for Manila Bay from San Jose Bay near Corregidor Island with a cargo of silver pesos.
1115: Anchored in berth twenty-seven in Manila Bay.

13th November
1010: A (LCM) came alongside to receive (600,000) silver pesos.

(LCM) departed for the beach to Commander of Salvage Group, Philippine Sea Frontier (SGPSF) to off load the cargo of silver, with security aboard.

1140: This date the ship received her orders to return to the United States, after a few days in drydock at Subic Bay, Luzon, in the Philippine Islands.

The Teak is now no longer involved with the recovery of the silver treasure. She gets underway for (4) days of dry dock time at Port Olongado, Subic Bay, Luzon, in the Philippine Islands.

14th November
She entered dry dock (ARD12) in Subic Bay, Luzon, in the Philippine Islands.

She left the (ARD-12) on the
19th November
She left (ARD-12) and after dry dock time she stayed in the Philippine Islands.

27th November 1945,
0630: The U.S.S. Elder (AN-20) gets underway for the United States. She left Guiuan Harbor, Samar, in the Philippine Islands.

Her route home is via the Marianas and Pearl Harbor, Territory of Hawaii Then to San Pedro harbor, Los Angles, California.

4th January 1946, she was tow to Astoria, in the state Washington, and was decommissioned 30th August 1946.

This closes the chapter on the U.S.S. Teak (AN-35) for her part in the recovery of the silver treasure at the bottom of Caballo Bay. Her total recovery of silver pesos was well over (2,000,000) Pesos.

It is now time to tell of the other Net Tender that will take over where the U.S. Teak left off and that ship is the U.S.S. Elder (AN-20) with (Lt) Joseph C. Patterson USN/R commanding.

The U.S.S. Elder (AN-20) being attached to (Ship Salvage, Fire Fighting, and Rescue Unit, Service Force Pacific) left Subic Bay, Luzon, in the Philippine Islands.

13th November
1106: The U.S.S. Elder (AN-20) in route to Manila Bay, Luzon, Philippine Islands.
1855: She drop anchor in the vicinity of berth 28, in Manila Bay, Luzon, Philippine Islands

14th November She gets underway to go alongside the U.S.S Teak (AN-35) for transfer diving gear and Navy and Army personnel to the Elder (AN-20), transferring of gear and personnel was completed at (1615), the U.S.S. Elder (AN-20) gets underway from alongside the Teak and heads for (berth 28) in Manila bay, Luzon, in the Philippine Islands.

The U.S.S. Elder (AN-20)

17th November
Still anchored in (berth 28), First (Lt.) C.W. Kimbal United States Army is transferred from the beach to the Elder as a security officer for the up and coming silver operation.

1300: On this day she gets underway for the silver site at Caballo Bay.

1910: She is moored to the mooring buoys at the silver site in Caballo Bay.

18th November

1000: The first dive begins. Starting the U.S.S. Elders (AN-20) part in the silver recovery operation at Caballo Bay. She remains on station recovering the treasure till she gets underway.

28th November

0710: Her heading is the inner harbor of Manila Bay.

1115: Anchoring in (berth 28) in Manila Bay and after all things are secured, the word is passed that at (1250) First (Lt.) C.W. Kimbel United States Army has completed his tour as security officer and is transferred back to his duty station on the beach at Ship Salvage, Fire Fighting and Rescue Unit, Service Force, Pacific (SGPSF). (Ship Salvage, Fire Fighting and Rescue Unit, Service Force, Pacific).

Then on the 1st of December 1945 the Elder is underway to return to the salvage site and begin diving operation. She arrives at the anchorage in Caballo Bay and completes the mooring at (1550) to the four mooring buoys. The U.S.S. Elder on December 2nd at (0824) again commenced diving operations to recover the silver treasure on the bottom of Caballo Bay. The diving operation continues till December 12th when at (1159) the U.S.S. Elder is underway for the inner harbor of Manila Bay. She arrives at the vicinity of (berth 29) in the inner harbor of Manila Bay at (1555). On the 14th of December she off loaded (26,125) pounds of silver pesos at a value of approximately (611,000) United States dollars, this being around (607,000) pesos. The pesos were delivered to First (Lt.) E.J. McKillop USA. Attached to (SGPSF).

(Note: the value of silver coins was determined by weighing (100) pounds of silver pesos. It took (2,339) pesos to make a (100 pounds).

(0720) December 17th, The U.S.S. Elder (AN-20) got underway for the anchorage at Caballo Bay to resume diving operations. Mooring is completed at the site at (1040) and the diving for silver is commenced. The diving operation continued till December 23rd when all diving stopped. The Elder (AN-20) gets underway for the inner harbor of Manila Bay, Luzon, in the Philippine Islands. (1220), arriving at (berth 29) Manila Bay, Luzon, in the Philippine Islands. The U.S.S. Elder (AN-20) observed Christmas on December 25th 1945, in Manila Bay, Luzon, Philippine Islands.

(0850) December 26th, The Elder delivered to (Lt) T.L. Samvelson USN/R attached to (SGPSF), (127) bags of silver pesos. Weighing approximately (12,930) pounds with a value of (302,613) pesos. After off loading the silver, the ship heads back to the silver recovery site in Caballo Bay, the mooring is completed by (1700) to the four mooring buoys.

Silver operation is continued till the 30th of December when she at (1105) gets underway for the inner Harbor of Manila Bay, Luzon, in the Philippine Islands. At (1635) ship anchored in (berth 28). Then she began to offload (57) bags of silver pesos with the approximate weigh of (4588) pounds. The silver is delivered to (Ens.) L.F. Beldson USN/R attached to (SGPSF).

On the 31st of December the U.S.S. Elder is ordered to Subic Bay, Luzon, Philippine Islands for dry dock time. At (0610) she is underway for Subic Bay and arriving in Subic Bay at (1505) then her heading is to (berth 206) and arriving at her berth at (1627). (1st January 1946, Happy New Year). The Elder stayed in (berth 206) till January 14th at (0749) she got underway and entered dry dock (AFD-28) at (0828) by (1020) she was resting on the cradle of the dry dock. Her stay in (AFD-28) lasted till January 17th, 1946. When at (0748) she left dry dock (AFT-28) and set course for (berth 206) in Subic Bay, Luzon, Philippine Islands.

At (1418) arriving at (berth 209), where she dropped anchor and stayed till she left (berth 209) and headed back to the silver site on January 20th.

(0637) Arriving at Caballo Bay at (1050) after mooring to the four mooring buoys the diving operation started. Diving stopped on the 29th of January. 29th Janurary the U.S.S. Elder (AN-20) is underway for Manila Bay to off load her silver she had recovered in Caballo Bay. 30th January at (0830) she off loaded (124) bags of silver pesos onto a (LCM). This is approximate (9,816 pounds), of silver that is off loaded into a (LCM). The silver cargo in (LCM) is turned over to (SGPSF). Receipted for by (Ens.) L.F. Bledso.

The Elder leaves Manila Bay,Luzon, Philippine Islands. At (0612) February 2nd her heading is back to the salvage site in Caballo Bay and by (1050) is moored to the four mooring buoys at the site. (1215) February 2nd The Elder starts the diving operation as before in Caballo Bay.

With no more general quarters since August 14th, 1945 the Elder is back on a peacetime routine. So when diving is stopped at different intervals it is to take on fuel, fresh water, and supplies, transfer or receive personnel or to deliver recovered silver pesos to Manila. So the story doesn't get boring to the reader a lot of routine activities will be left out of the story and only insert things that are interesting.

February 2nd to 15th February 1946, The U.S.S. Elder (AN-20) recovered (155) bags of silver pesos, weighing approximately (13,267) pounds and delivered the pesos to (SGPSF) on the 15th of February to Lt (jg) L.F. Bledsoe USN/R attached to (SGPSF) Manila. No March 4th, the Elder transferred under armed guard to (SGPSF) approximately 300,000 pesos or 150 bags, weighing approximately (12,886) pounds. Then 18th March at (1002) transferred (170) bags of silver pesos, weighing (14,124) pounds, was transferred to the custody of (Lt.) R.J. Norman USN attached to (SGPSF). Then on April 1st another transfer was made to the custody of (Lt.) R.J. Norman (123) bags of silver pesos, weighing (9,149) pounds and again on the 16th April another transfer of silver to (Lt.) Norman attached to (SGPSF) another (56) bags of silver pesos, weighing approximately (4,292) pounds.

16th April
1030: The U.S.S. Elder (AN-20) got underway for Subic Bay, Luzon, Philippine Islands, by orders from the Commander of Salvage Group, Philippine Sea Frontier. Arriving Subic Bay at (1735) and by (1827) she was anchored in (berth 206).

17th April
(1300) While still anchored in (berth 206) all hands to quarters for change of command ceremonies. With all hands at quarters the

reading of the orders is Lt. J.C. Patterson USN/R commanding officer and to receive the command of the Elder is Ens. Robert C. Olson USN/R. Before taking command of the Elder, Ensign Olson was the Executive Officer, Navigator and also severed as the (1st) Lieutenant. (1525) Lt. J.C. Patterson UNS/R with new orders departed the U.S.S. Elder (AN-20) for transportation to the United States, for ultimate discharge from the United States Navy.

It is time to insert some trivia that in some ways affected the silver recovery in Caballo Bay after August 15, 1945.

If you look at the records of all services after that date in August you will see a transfer of a great number of personnel took place. The transfers through out all of the services are being transferred through a program set up by the government (to release all personnel that was a reserve or drafted etc).

The personnel exempted from this program were all regular enlisted personnel and officers.

The program is called the point system and it started at the end of the war in Europe.
In this program when it started you needed (85) points to be transferred home. If you did not meet the required points you were assigned to a new unit and stayed in Europe or were transferred to the Pacific area. In Europe your assignment would be in the occupation service. The number of points you needed to go home after August 15th 1945, in the Pacific area was (75) points.
Points were awarded for the following.
1) +1 point for each month of service.
   (Between 16th of September 1940 to August 15th 1945)
2) +1 point for each month overseas.
   (Between September 16th 1940 to August 15th 1945)
3) +5 points for each award received: DSC, LM, SS, DFC, SM, BS, AM, and the PH.
4) +5 points for every campaign stars worn on a theater ribbon.

5) +12 points for each child (under 18) up to a limit of (3) children.

If you were in the pacific area and did not qualify you stayed on station or were assigned to another unit as occupation service. The ones with no kids or the younger men without any families had to stay onboard.

Also many of all the service personnel fit into the above program. Which made all operations in all areas very difficult to keep on track. This is why the U.S.S. Teak, U.S.S. Elder had such a turn over in personnel since August 15th, 1945 for many of the ships company were qualified to go back to the United States. But for lack of points, it would be months before some could return home.

April 17th to April 27th The U.S.S. Elder (AN-20) stayed at anchor in Subic Bay and carried out her daily shipboard routine, although she had to make some berth changes. Leaving Subic Bay on the 27th at (0556) under the command of Ensign R.L. Olson USN/R. The U.S.S. Elder (AN-20) arrives back in Manila Bay, Luzon, in the Philippine Islands. At (berth 29) at (1357). (0830) Underway to the silver site in Caballo Bay, and moored to the buoys at (0950). (1010) the diving operation starts. The diving continues till May 2nd when by authority of Bupers dispatch, (Lt.) Charles S. Moberly, USN reported aboard and assumed command of the U.S.S. Elder (AN-20). Then on May 10th at (1045) she is underway for Manila Bay, Luzon, in the Philippine Islands, to (berth 27) arriving at (1402). May 11th she offloaded (70) bags of silver pesos. Approximate weight of (5,415) pounds. This load of silver pesos is transferred to (SGPSF) and this being the last recorded transfer of silver. 14th May at (0530) she heads back to Caballo Bay where she arrives at (0910), where she ties to one mooring buoy with a cable from the stern and then drops her starboard bow anchor. Diving starts at (0935), she then on the 15th May, gets underway to shift the four mooring buoys to a new location. Completing the moving of the mooring buoys at (1535).

16th May
0630: Commenced diving operation and secured at (1150).

By records:
16th of May 10,000 pesos recovered.
17th of May 21,000 pesos recovered
21st of May 21,000 pesos recovered
22nd of May No pesos recovered

The 23rd May

0815: The U.S.S. Elder (AN-20) secured diving operations for the last time with no pesos found. 0845: The U.S.S. elder (AN-20) leaves Caballo Bay, for the last time and heads back to (berth 27) in Manila Bay, Luzon, Philippine Islands. The U.S.S. Elder (AN-20) her total recovery of silver pesos and including the (52,000) pesos is about (3,000,000) pesos total. There is no record of the U.S.S. Elder (AN-20) offloading the (52,000) silver pesos she recovered after May 23rd to (SGPSF). It could be an oversight on the part of the officer on watch at the time of the offloading in Manila Bay, Luzon, in the Philippine Islands. There is no entry of the date or time when all Army and Navy personnel or diving gear was transferred back to Commander Salvage Group, Philippine Sea Frontier. This brings to the end, the silver operation for the Navy and Army in Caballo Bay.

The U.S.S. Elder (AN-20) although done with the silver operations in May of 1946. She was ordered to Subic Bay, Luzon, in the Philippine Islands. Where the ships new base of operations would take place. Here she was assigned numerous jobs like assisting in decommissioning small craft; maintained moorings; transported passengers and cargo between Philippine ports; and occasionally escorted small craft to Okinawa.

The U.S.S. Elder (AN-20) returned to the United States in August 3rd 1948. Arriving at Naval depot at Tiburon, California for duty till 23rd of May 1949, when she sailed for Alaskan waters for various duties. Returning to Tiburon, California on 13th of October 1949 for duty. Then March of 1950 was ordered to the western Pacific, when on 11th of March a week out of Pearl Harbor, Territory of Hawaii.

A serious fire broke out in the engine room. With all headway lost and no water pressure, the U.S.S. Elder (AN-20) appeared doomed.

But sound training and Navy "know how," and with combined courage in the ship's intrepid damage control parties, subdued the flames. Her engines damaged beyond repair, the stricken Net Tender drifted helplessly for a week before assistance in the form of the U.S.S. Comstock (LSD-19) and the U.S.S. Piedmont (AD-17) arriving on March 18th.

She was taken in tow by the U.S.S. Deliver (ARS-23) and began the long slow haul to Pearl Harbor, Territory of Hawaii. Her extensive repairs completed The U.S.S. Elder (AN-20) sailed from Pearl Harbor, Territory of Hawaii to 26th January 1951, for operation in Yokosuka Japan, for an operating base in the Korean War. From Japan she is sent back to Tiburon California to operate again all over the Pacific area.

Then she is assigned to the 13th Naval District in April 1954, for training duty with the harbor defense unit of the Pacific Northwest, from this duty station. She was decommissioned on 18th December 1959. Being in service from 12th November 1941 the U.S.S. Elder (AN-20) with close to 18 years of service. The U.S.S. Elder (AN-20) served the United States Navy all over the East Coast, and the Pacific. She battled all kinds of weather, the war in the Atlantic and Pacific, doing many different jobs.

So ends a very short story on the secret silver recovery of Caballo Bay, Manila Bay, Luzon, in the Philippine Islands.

"We in the Navy have a blue suit waiting for anyone who can wear it. This suit is cut from the fabric of freedom, and is tailored to the lean and form-fitting style of dedicated purpose set for us by our founding father. I don't expect it ever to go out of fashion. But it can if not enough men and women are willing to wear it with pride and respect". (By George W. Anderson Jr.)

When you look on a map at the location of the silver pesos that lay on the bottom of Caballo Bay, the location falls in the South Channel to the entrance of Manila Bay just off Caballo Island and off the tail of Corregidor Island, which has the look of a pollywog. At this location the condition for working on the bottom is treacherous,

with the currents and the silver pesos lying in boxes and with some
already broken open and the loose silver lying in the silt on the
bottom of the channel. With this kind of working condition it is far
less glamorous as the books and movies make it out to be. You are
fighting currents, visibility, darkness, mud and sea grass and keeping
a look out for unfriendly sea creatures, also keeping a eye on your air
lines from getting fouled and to top it off you can only stay on the
bottom for thirty minutes at 20 fathoms plus or minus and another
35 minutes to get back to the surface from the floor of Caballo Bay.

Between the Japanese effort in 1942 and the efforts of the U.S.
Navy in 1945 and 1946 approximately (7,000,000) million pesos had
been recovered at the time the Philippines gained their independence.
This is only one-half or less than half of the total silver originally
dumped in Caballo Bay South of Corregidor. Since that time only
a small portion of the remainder, has been recovered. The most
successful of these various operations, performed under contract with
the Philippine Government, occurred in 1947 when two American
divers pooled their resources, outfitted a barge, and employed several
of the Moro's who had dived with the (9) American prisoners of war
in 1942. After firing the Moro's for stealing the few pesos that were
being brought to the surface, they found a pile of boxes that were
filled with silver pesos just as their funds were nearly exhausted. The
amount of silver recovered has not been disclosed, but speculation has
it at about (500,000) pesos.

More than four million dollars in silver still lies on the floor of
Caballo Bay. Scattered and buried by the currents and storms of
years, it will probably remain there forever- a watery monument to
the first Navy divers who did their best to try and keep it there.

"In years to come, when sailors are home from the sea, they will
still remember with fondness and respect the ocean in all its moods-
the impossible shimmering mirror calm and the storm-tossed green
water surging over the bow. And then there will come again a faint
whiff of stack gas, a faint echo of engine and rudder orders, a vision
of the bright bunting of signal flags snapping at the yardarm, a refrain

of hearty laughter in the wardroom and chief's quarters and mess decks. Gone ashore for good they will grow wistful about their Navy days, when the seas belonged to them and a new port of call was ever over the horizon. Remembering this, they will stand taller and say, "I WAS A SAILOR ONCE. I WAS PART OF THE NAVY, AND THE NAVY WILL ALWAYS BE PART OF ME." This is the last paragraph of " I WAS A SAILOR ONCE" (Reflection of a blackshoe) By Vice Admiral Harold Koenig USN (Ret), M.D.

"I find the great thing in this world is not so much where we stand, as in what direction we are moving: to reach the part of heaven, we must sail sometimes with the wind and sometimes against it, -- but we must sail, and not drift, nor lie at anchor" By Oliver Wendell Holmes Sr.

Always save the best for last, for this should cover almost everyone in the above story. For the poem covers it all.

Navy Poem

By

Lt. JG Don Ballard

Come gather round me lads and I'll tell you a thing or two,
about the way we ran the Navy in forty-two.

When wooden ships and iron men were barley out of sight,
I am going to give you some facts just to set the record right.

We wore the ole bellbottoms, with a flat hat on our head,
and we always hit the sack at night. We never "went to bed."

Our uniforms were worn ashore, and we were might proud.
Never though of wearing civvies, in fact they were not allowed.

Now when a ship puts out to sea. I'll tell you son-it hurts! When
suddenly you notice that half the crew wearing SKIRTS. And it's
hard for me to imagine, a female boatswains mate, stopping on the
quarterdeck to make sure her stockings are straight.

What happen to KiYi brush, and the salt-water bath,
Holy stoning decks at night-cause you stirred up old Bosn's wrath!

We always had our gedunk stand and lots of pogey bait.
And it always took a hitch or two, just to make rate.

In your seabag all your skivvies, were neatly stopped and rolled.
And the blankets on your sack had better have a three-inch fold.

Your little ditty bag, it is hard to believe just how much it held,
and you wouldn't go ashore with pants that hadn't been spiked and
belled.

We had scullery maids and succotash and good old S.O.S.
and when you felt like topping off-you headed for the mess.

Oh we had our belly robbers-but there weren't to many grips.
For the deck apes were never hungry and there were no staring snipes.

Now you never hear of Davey Jones, Shellbacks Or Polliwogs,
and you never splice the mainbrace to receive your daily grog.

Now you never have to dog a watch or stand the main event.
You even tie your lines today – back in my time they were bent.

We were two-fisted drinkers and no one though you sinned, if you
staggered back aboard your ship, three sheets to the wind. And with just
a couple of hours of sleep you regained your usual luster. Bright eyed
and bushy tailed-you still made morning muster.

Rocks and Shoals have long since gone, and now it's U.C.M.J.
Back then the old man handled everything if you should go astray.

Now they steer the ship with dials, and I wouldn't be surprised,
if some day they sail the dammed thing-from the beach computerized.

So when my earthly hitch is over, and the good Lord picks the best, I'll
walk right up to him and say, "Sir, I have but one request-let me sail the
seas of Heaven in a coat of Navy Blue. Like I did so long ago on earth-
way back in nineteen-forty two."

The End

References

1) The book ("One Man's War" Diving as a Quest of the Emperor) by R.C. Sheats USN Ret. (USN master diver)
2) U.S. Naval Institute Proceedings magazine of March 1958. Article (Japanese Treasure Hunt in Manila Bay) by Commander W.L. Marshall, USN
3) Life Magazine of October 15th 1945. Article (Sunken-Treasure Hunt) by Life staff writer
4) Reader's Digest April 1959. Article (The Great Manila Bay Silver Operation) by John G. Hubbell
5) Army magazine "YANK" November 2nd 1945 Vol.4, No.20. Article (Silver Hunt) By Army staff writer.
6) National Archives and Records Administration
   8601 Adelphi Road
   College Park, Maryland 20740-6001
7) Department of the Navy
   Naval Historical Center
   805 Kidder Breese St. SE
Washington Navy Yard, DC 20374-5060
8) http://www.hazegray.org
9) http://history.navy.mil
10) "WORLD WAR 11" magazine for July 2000. Article "The Great Philippine Silver Odyssey" by William P. Endicott.
11) http:// en.wikipedia.org
12) "CORREGIDOR" The Treasure Island of WW11, By Edward Michaud (part 1 and 2).
13) Ships Log of the U.S.S. Teak AN35.
14) Ships Log of the U.S.S. Elder AN20.
15) The Muster Roll of the crew of the U.S.S. Pigeon (ARS-6) (Minesweeper) From March 1939 to February 1942.
16) The Muster Roll of the crew of the U.S.S. Canopus (AS-9) (Submarine Tender) From March 1939 to February 1942.
17) www.google.com
18) www.yahoo.com

19) http://corregidor.org/chs_calmes/usamp_harrison.htm
20) Book "Reminiscences" by General of the Army (Douglas MacArthur)
21) Milton Meechan (Moose) RM 2/c, served aboard the U.S.S. Teak (AN-35) during world war two and at the time of the silver recovery. Living now in Newport Beach, California.